Into the Long War

Oxford Research Group (ORG) is an independent non-governmental organisation which seeks to bring about positive change on issues of national and international security. Established in 1982, it is now considered to be one of the UK's leading think tanks on international affairs. ORG is a registered charity and uses a combination of innovative publications, expert roundtables, residential consultations, and engagement with opinion-formers, to develop and promote alternative global security strategies. <www.oxfordresearchgroup.org.uk>

Into the Long War

Oxford Research Group
International Security Report 2006

Paul Rogers

Pluto Press

LONDON • ANN ARBOR, MI

First published 2007 by Pluto Press
345 Archway Road, London N6 5AA
and 839 Greene Street, Ann Arbor, MI 48106

www.plutobooks.com

British Library Cataloguing in Publication Data
A catalogue record for this book is available from the British Library

Hardback
ISBN-13   978 0 7453 2612 2
ISBN-10   0 7453 2612 9

Paperback
ISBN-13   978 0 7453 2611 5
ISBN-10   0 7453 2611 0

Library of Congress Cataloging in Publication Data applied for

10 9 8 7 6 5 4 3 2 1

Designed and produced for Pluto Press by
Chase Publishing Services Ltd, Fortescue, Sidmouth, EX10 9QG, England
Typeset from disk by Stanford DTP Services, Northampton, England
Printed and bound in the European Union by
Antony Rowe Ltd, Chippenham and Eastbourne, England

Contents

Introduction

In October 2002, Oxford Research Group published an analysis of the possible effects of a US attack on the Saddam Hussein regime – *Iraq: Consequences of a War*.[1] The report pointed to the likely impact of an occupation of Iraq on regional antagonism to the United States extending even to increased support for the al-Qaida movement and also pointed to the risk of a developing insurgency.

Oxford Research Group was far from being alone in expressing these concerns, but the war went ahead and the Saddam Hussein regime was terminated in barely three weeks. Within a further few weeks there were already clear signs of developing instability in Iraq, demonstrated in two different ways. One was the immediate deterioration in public order, with the onset of widespread looting that could not be contained by the coalition troops that had replaced the old regime. The other was the outbreak of attacks on the coalition troops themselves, especially US forces in Baghdad and Central Iraq. Even as President Bush was making his famous 'mission accomplished' speech on the flight deck of the aircraft carrier USS *Abraham Lincoln*, on 1 May 2003, American, British and other coalition forces were already involved in counter-insurgency operations.

It therefore looked as though the Iraq War was still in its early stages, rather than being a brief conflict, and Afghanistan, too, was experiencing a degree of violence and disorder that suggested that here was another zone of conflict that might not make the transition to peace and security that had been so confidently expected in 2002. In these circumstances, Oxford Research Group commenced a series of International Security Monthly Briefings in May 2003, that were intended to analyse the major developments in the 'war on terror', while endeavouring to put these developments in a long-term context.

The core of the present volume comprises those briefings produced from May 2005 to April 2006, and is the third such volume. It analyses what was essentially the third year of the current Iraq War, while also discussing the evolving conflict in Afghanistan, increasing tensions with Iran, incidents of paramilitary violence related to the al-Qaida movement, and developments in US, British and coalition military postures. The briefings are reproduced here with a minimum of editing, this being confined to minor matters of grammatical improvement or the avoidance of repetition. They are placed in context in the first chapter with a review of developments from September 2001 through to April 2005, and there is an extensive final chapter that places the year from May 2005 to April 2006 in a longer-term context. In particular, this focuses on the transition from a terminology of a 'war on terror' to a 'long war', with the latter suggesting that the post-9/11 global security environment is likely to take the form of an enduring conflict stretching well beyond a decade.

In February 1993, President Clinton's new appointee as Director of Central Intelligence, James Woolsey, had characterised the transition to the post-Cold War world as being one in which the United States had slain the dragon but now lived in a jungle full of poisonous snakes. Thirteen years later, and five years after the 9/11 attacks, the taming of that jungle is seen as the main task of the US military for the foreseeable future. The first year of the Iraq War was one in which liberation turned to occupation and then to insurgency, and the second year saw the consolidation of that insurgency coupled with renewed insecurity in Afghanistan. The third

year has seen the development of an attitude within the United
States that sees a long-term conflict ahead even though this
has coincided with a marked decrease in political support for
the war in Iraq. If a 'long war' does ensue, then the period
covered by this report will mark that further transition, with
implications that may be felt for some decades.

A Note on Sources

Oxford Research Group's monthly international security
briefings are written using a wide range of sources and, in
this volume, a number of the more specific of these are given
in the endnotes. The briefings have tended to involve a degree
of critical analysis that is in marked contrast to the outlooks
and expectations persistently expressed by the Bush and Blair
administrations, and they have tended to be substantially more
accurate in their prognosis over the past three years. It might
therefore be useful to indicate some of the sources used.

In what might be termed the mainstream media, US, UK
and French broadsheets are accessed, commonly on a daily
basis, with the *Washington Post, New York Times, Boston
Globe, Los Angeles Times, Financial Times, Guardian* and
Le Monde being particularly useful. Newspapers in Israel,
Pakistan and India are also useful as are broadcast news
media websites for the BBC, Al-Jazeera, CNN and others.
Elements of the defence press are valuable sources, with *Jane's
Defence Weekly, Aviation Week and Space Technology, Jane's
Intelligence Review, Jane's International Defence Review*
and *Defence News* being particularly useful. The British Aid
to Afghanistan Group's monthly assessment is invariably
pertinent as are the Institute for War and Peace Reporting's
Iraq Crisis Reports.

Some individual websites are of consistent help, especially
Juan Cole's *Informed Comment,* and William J. Arkin's site at
the *Washington Post.* Some of the *Strategic Comments* from

the International Institute of Strategic Studies in London have proved both useful and prescient, and Anthony Cordesman's reports published by the Center for International and Strategic Studies in Washington are always worth studying. These are some of the most helpful examples of sources, to which may be added many blogs, especially those originating in Iraq, whether from Iraqis, from coalition troops or others.

Beyond this, though, have been that wide range of individuals, including many senior military officers, who have been willing to discuss the issues covered here, often informally and on the occasion of conferences, seminars or lectures. In the year covered by this book, they have included sessions at Chatham House, the Royal United Services Institute, the Joint Service Command and Staff College, the Defence Concepts and Doctrine Centre, the Institute for Regional Studies in Islamabad, the Institute for Political and International Studies in Tehran and the UN University for Peace in Costa Rica. In addition, Oxford Research Group's own staff and wide range of contacts have proved invaluable.

Acknowledgements

I would like to thank the Director of Oxford Research Group, Professor John Sloboda, and members of staff for assistance and ideas in the production of this report, especially Chris Abbott for his work in ensuring the production and distribution of the monthly analyses that form a core part of this annual report. The origins of this report lie with Dr Scilla Elworthy who originally proposed the idea of regular analytical briefings for Oxford Research Group following the start of the Iraq War in March 2003, and their development has been aided by a number of discussions hosted by Gabrielle Rifkind. More generally, I would like to thank many scores of people who have contributed indirectly to the analysis in this report, including peace-workers, military personnel, journalists, academics and others, as well as hosts in countries visited during the year covered by this report including Iran, Pakistan and the United States.

1
The Context for a Long War

Following the election of President George W. Bush in November 2000, United States foreign and security policy was heavily influenced by the neo-conservative outlook and the belief that the United States had a unique role in evolving an international economic and political system that was effectively in the American image. A combination of free market economics and western-style democratic governance was seen as the only way forward now that the Soviet Union was long gone and even China was embracing major elements of the market economy. While this idea of a New American Century was never accepted across the whole American political spectrum it was particularly prominent in neo-conservative thinking and the early months of the Bush administration saw much of this outlook reflected in policy changes.

These included opposition to a number of multilateral agreements, including the Comprehensive Test Ban Treaty and the Anti-Ballistic Missile Treaty, and a markedly critical approach to negotiations on the International Criminal Court and the strengthening of the 1972 Biological and Toxin Weapons Convention. Perhaps of most surprise to some European allies was the decision to withdraw from the Kyoto Climate Change Protocols, but this should not have been so unexpected given the firm belief of the new administration that the United States should not be constrained by international

agreements that were not clearly in its own interest, whatever
the global context.

As Charles Krauthammer put it in June 2001:

> Multipolarity, yes, when there is no alternative. But not when there
> is. Not when we have the unique imbalance of power that we enjoy
> today – and that has given the international system a stability and
> essential tranquillity it had not known for at least a century.
>
> The international environment is far more likely to enjoy peace
> under a single hegemon. Moreover, we are not just any hegemon.
> We run a uniquely benign imperium.[1]

Responding to the 9/11 Attacks

By September 2001, this approach was firmly established within
US security thinking in the Bush administration and there was
considerable confidence that the United States had the military
and economic power coupled with political influence to ensure
that it remained the world leader in the new century. In such
a context the 9/11 atrocities came as a severe shock and the
reaction was immediate and forceful. Within three months
the Taliban regime in Afghanistan had been terminated by
military action, on the grounds that the regime harboured key
leadership elements of the al-Qaida movement that was held
responsible for the 9/11 attacks.

The termination of the Taliban was achieved not by the use
of substantial US ground forces but by a combination of the
extensive use of air power, the employment of Special Forces
and, most notably, by the rapid re-arming and support of the
Northern Alliance. In taking this latter path, the United States
effectively altered the balance of power in the ongoing Afghan
civil war, ensuring the rapid demise of the Taliban, even though
most elements melted away, often with weapons intact. That
the Taliban did not suffer a comprehensive and irreversible
military defeat was not recognised at the time, even if there
was severe fighting in the Tora Bora mountain region within
months of the fall of Kabul.

In the early part of 2002 there were urgent calls from UN and other specialists for substantial aid for Afghanistan, not just in terms of extensive development assistance but also through the provision of large numbers of peace-keeping troops to play a stabilising role. Expert assessments pointed to the need for up to 30,000 military and police personnel, but barely 5,000 were provided to form the International Security Assistance Force (ISAF). In a separate operation, the United States established two major military bases in Afghanistan – at Bagram, north of Kabul, and at Kandahar. While the initial intention was to constitute these as permanent bases with relatively small numbers of troops, by the latter part of 2002 insurgent activity was developing to the extent that the United States was committing many thousands of combat troops to face a developing if initially small-scale insurgency.

Meanwhile, and following the regime termination in Afghanistan, President Bush's State of Union address in January 2002 extended the war on terror to encompass an 'axis of evil' of regimes that supported terrorism and were also intent on developing weapons of mass destruction, especially nuclear weapons. Iraq, Iran and North Korea were named as primary members of this axis of evil. Mr Bush subsequently made it clear that the United States had the right to pre-empt threats from states or sub-state actors before such threats against the United States were realised. During the early months of 2002, Iraq was singled out as being the most immediate threat to US security interests in the Middle East, with suggestions that the Saddam Hussein regime's support for terrorist movements might even mean there was an indirect threat from Iraq to the continental United States.

During the course of the latter part of 2002, a coalition of supporting states was assembled for the purpose of regime termination in Iraq. The eventual group of states was smaller than the coalition assembled in 1990–91 after the Iraqi occupation of Kuwait, even though a degree of approval was sought from the United Nations. The United States provided the great majority of troops, aircraft and ships, although Britain was also significant when compared with other states such as Australia and Italy that sent modest contingents.

The military operation to terminate the Saddam Hussein regime began in March 2003, with the regime falling within three weeks. The expectation was that US and other coalition troops would be welcomed as liberators across much of Iraq, a friendly government would be established in Baghdad, would develop a free market economy and would look to the United States for security. Within three weeks of the end of the Saddam Hussein regime there were reports that the United States would establish four permanent military sites in Iraq, with perhaps 20,000 personnel based there. In the short term, though, it was expected that the 150,000 troops involved in the initial occupation would be scaled down to 70,000 within six months. It is worth noting, though, that some assessments by analysts in the United States and elsewhere believed that there was a prospect of an insurgency and that several hundred thousand troops might be required to ensure security.

The Iraq War – Year One

The initial success in terminating the Saddam Hussein regime disguised a number of problems and issues that were present from the very start of the war, even before President Bush declared military operations successful in his USS *Abraham Lincoln* speech on 1 May 2003. There had originally been considerable confidence that the 'shock and awe' of a major air assault would make it relatively easy for highly mobile ground troops to move rapidly forward to Baghdad, even though Turkey had refused to allow US troops to enter from the north. There was even a belief in some quarters that the Saddam Hussein regime would collapse in the face of the initial air assault.

From the very start of the war, though, there was an unexpected level of resistance, not so much from regular troops in armoured formations in open country but from irregular or paramilitary units operating mainly in urban environments. It took several days to take control of the small but strategically significant port of Umm Qasr, close to the Kuwait border, and as US troops began to move towards Baghdad they found a constant problem of attacks on supply lines by irregular forces. Furthermore, the first incidents of suicide bombings against US troops occurred within two weeks of the start of the war.[2]

In spite of these problems, the main US force progressed towards Baghdad rapidly and was able to use a combination of intensive air power and ground artillery to damage hugely the regular Republican Guard formations that formed a defensive shield to the south of Baghdad. There had been an expectation that the city itself would be heavily defended, possibly by the elite Special Republican Guard, together with *fedayeen* and commando units and the troop formations attached to the regime's various security and intelligence agencies. In practice, the defences were minimal apart from some intensive conflict close to the international airport, and the regime fell quickly. The deceptive part of this rapid process, though, was that an absence of resistance by elite units did not equate with their defeat.

Two other issues were relevant in the first month of the war. One was that there was a minimum of rejoicing by Iraqis at the fall of the old regime, except in the Kurdish North East. While a positive reaction had not been expected in many of the Sunni population areas of central Iraq, there had been an expectation of welcome in the Shi'a population centres in southern Iraq and in parts of Baghdad. This simply did not happen. Possible explanations at the time included the memory of the failure of the United States to support the Shi'a uprising after the first Iraq War in 1991, together with the possible continued presence of influential regime elements in the towns and cities of the south. Even allowing for these factors, the lack of immediate support for the occupying powers was a major surprise, with the prowess of the United States military also badly affected by its inability to control the comprehensive breakdown of law and order and especially the widespread looting that developed within days of the regime's demise.

Within three months of the end of the old regime, it was apparent that armed resistance to the coalition presence was beginning in earnest. In July 2003 alone, the US forces lost 48 troops killed and several hundred wounded and in the year from 1 May 2003, the day in which Bush had declared victory, US forces were to lose 601 people killed and some 3,000 seriously wounded.

Three of the early factors aiding the developing insurgency became apparent. One was that many Iraqis, especially among Sunni communities, were resentful of what was seen from the start not as liberation but as foreign occupation, an aspect made worse by the immediate decline in living standards in the face of a wide range of shortages. A second was that many of the elite forces that were loyal to the old regime had survived the first few weeks of the war almost unscathed, having largely melted away rather than face US forces with their massive advantages in firepower. These elements recognised that many of the senior figures in the Saddam Hussein regime were killed or detained in the early weeks of the occupation, but Saddam Hussein and his two sons survived. Aiding the developing insurgency was the third factor – the dispersal and ready availability of large quantities of arms and munitions.

During the course of the period May 2003 to June 2004, Iraq was run by the Coalition Provisional Authority (CPA) under the leadership of Paul Bremer. The CPA moved rapidly to encourage a market economy but failed to prevent considerable damage to the physical infrastructure of the country, either from looters or insurgents. The oil industry and electricity production and distribution were badly affected, even in the first year, but two other matters added to the CPA's problems. One was an intensive programme of 'de-Ba'athification', as elements in public service that had been connected to the former Ba'ath Party were removed from office. Since many of them were technocrats with little more than the nominal party membership necessary for survival under the old regime, the effect was to deprive the country of substantial elements of the human resources necessary for reconstruction and development.

The second CPA error was the remarkable decision to disband the old Iraqi Army. Even though many of the 400,000 personnel had deserted or been stood down by their officers in the early weeks of the conflict, their dismissal meant that large numbers of soldiers were thrust into unemployment, producing an embittered cohort from which insurgents could gain further recruits.

By August 2003, a series of attacks, including the bombing of the UN offices in Baghdad, demonstrated the power of the insurgency. Even so, there appeared to be an enduring belief in the CPA and among the US military that the attacks were due simply to discontented 'remnants' of the old regime and would fade away rapidly. These could be seen as terrorists, with Iraq now being seen as a key focus for the wider war on terror.

The deaths of Qusay and Uday Hussein in Mosul in July 2003 and the subsequent detention of Saddam Hussein himself five months later were both expected to blunt the insurgency, but neither incident had any discernible effect. Moreover, it was apparent by early 2004 that insurgents had consolidated control of some towns and cities in central Iraq. During April 2004, much of the focus was on Fallujah where attempts to secure the city following the killing of four American contractors resulted in intensive violence, with US forces trying to take control in the face of considerable resistance and high casualties. In that month alone, the US forces had 135 of its troops killed.

The Iraq War – Year Two

As the war entered its second year, there continued to be optimism within the Bush administration that the insurgency would wind down. Much was made of the entry into Iraq of some jihadist paramilitaries from other countries across the region, with this being seen as proof that Iraq was becoming a prime theatre in the war on terror. In practice, the numbers were small – never more than one tenth of the total, but in some circles in Washington, Iraq was seen as a magnet for al-Qaida paramilitaries. It was, according to this view, hugely preferable that such terrorists would face up to overwhelming US military force under circumstances dictated by the Pentagon rather than concentrate on engaging in attacks on the United States or US interests abroad.

At the same time, during the course of the period May 2004 to April 2005, there were few signs of any improvement in the security situation in Afghanistan, and the al-Qaida movement remained active across the world, with attacks in Djakarta and Sinai. Moreover, US forces suffered continuing casualties in Iraq, including 851 people killed and almost 9,500 wounded. Of the latter, more than half were sufficiently wounded to be unable to return to duty within 72 hours, with many of these evacuated from Iraq to the Landstuhl military hospital in Germany and then onwards to the United States. In addition, many thousands of military personnel were evacuated back to the United States for treatment for non-combat injuries or mental or physical illness.

During this period, the impact of injuries became one of the defining if largely unrecognised features of the war. In most forms of modern conventional war, the ratio of injuries to deaths tends to be of the order of 3:1, whereas for the US military in Iraq it has tended to be around double that. There are two main reasons for this. One is that very high standards of battlefield medicine, especially the rapid stabilisation of casualties, means that far more people survive injuries that in other circumstances would kill them. The second is that the development and use of anti-ballistic body armour has meant that fatal injuries are less frequent. The effect of these two factors is to produce a situation in which many military personnel survive with serious injuries to the groin, face, head and throat and suffer limb injuries that frequently require amputation. This trend has had two impacts in terms of attitudes to the war, one in the United States and the other with the US military deployed in Iraq.

Regarding the domestic impact, the context is that the Bush administration has been reluctant to see its senior personnel connected with the issue of casualties. It has been rare for leading political figures to visit casualties in the military hospitals in the Washington area and little publicity has been given to the return home for burial of the soldiers killed in the war. Against this, though, the stream of funerals or the return to the towns and city districts across the United States of seriously injured young soldiers has had a slow but steady impact. There may be little national coverage, but local media outlets have reported on individual cases, with this in turn leading to a questioning of policy.

In relation to military attitudes in Iraq, the deaths and serious injuries suffered by US military personnel engaged in fighting an increasingly bitter urban insurgency resulted in an increasingly aggressive series of responses. The tendency has been to use the immense firepower advantage at any early stage in any insurgency attack on troops. Thus an individual sniper attack might stimulate a response involving many hundreds of rounds of ammunition or even the calling in of helicopter gun-ships or strike aircraft. Inevitably, a result has been high levels of civilian casualties among ordinary people caught up in the conflict, with deaths among civilians being at least ten times as high as those among the US military, a consequence being further antagonism to occupation.

If the issue of deaths and injuries to US troops was increasingly significant during the second year of the Iraq War, several other factors became more relevant. One was the level of Iraqi civilian casualties, which reached some 25,000 killed and tens of thousands of injured in the first two years. These estimates stem from external analysis, particularly the Iraq Body Count group, that draws its data primarily from multiple media sources.[3] Using an exacting media-based methodology gives reliable baseline figures but is also likely to underestimate total casualties due to under-reporting in the media. Consequently the figure of 25,000 casualties may actually be a marked underestimate of the true figure.

A second factor was the continued failure of the Iraq Survey Group to uncover any substantive evidence of the Saddam Hussein regime's retaining an active programme to develop nuclear, chemical or biological weapons. Indeed this was such a clear-cut outcome that the issue of weapons of mass destruction receded into the background as a reason for the war. This may have been one reason for the increased opposition to the war, especially in Western Europe, but it also serves to explain why the Bush administration was more insistent on linking the Iraq War with the wider al-Qaida movement. By doing this, a strong connection could be maintained between the difficult military task for US forces in Iraq and the original 9/11 attacks. Controlling the insurgency could be presented as a major response to 9/11.

Within Iraq, direct military support for the US forces from coalition partners eased substantially during 2004–05. Poland, Ukraine, and especially Britain maintained substantial troop numbers, but many small contingents were either withdrawn or were not replaced at the time of the rotation of units, and some significant contributors to the coalition such as Spain withdrew all their troops.

Against this, one relationship developed further: the military connection between the United States and Israel. This was direct in terms of the presence of Israeli military specialists working in the Kurdish areas of north-east Iraq on military training missions, but went much further than this in other respects. In much of Iraq the US forces were facing a vigorous insurgency for which they were not fully trained or equipped. In responding to this predicament, they found it particularly useful to link with the Israeli Defence Force and with Israeli arms companies, given their long experience of attempting to control dissent in the occupied territories of Palestine.

The US Army's Training and Doctrine Command (TRADOC) worked closely with Israeli counterparts, and the US Army as a whole made considerable use of specialised equipment developed in Israel for the control of the Palestinians. This included vehicle protection against rocket-propelled grenades and a wide range of surveillance equipment. Although the connection between the United States and Israel received little attention in the western media, it was a factor in the regional Middle Eastern coverage of the war that was much more prominent. As such, it was not difficult for propagandists to represent the relationship as one of neo-Christian forces linking with Zionists to control a major Arab country.

The differences between the regional media and the western media in the coverage of events in Iraq were also notable in two other respects. One was the coverage of civilian casualties. Apart from specialist groups such as Iraq Body Count, western media outlets only tended to cover the high incidence of Iraqi civilian casualties on the occasions of major incidents, with considerable self-censorship of the more graphic images of the dead and injured. Reputable regional outlets such as the Al-Jazeera and Al-Arabiya satellite television news channels were far more consistent in showing the ongoing effects of the war.

Media coverage also does much to explain the differing reactions to the issue of prisoner abuse. The Abu Ghraib issue raised major concerns in the United States and in Europe, with much analysis and comment in the print and broadcast media. The impression may have been given that it was not representative of the detention system in Iraq overall, but it still did damage to the Bush administration's standing over the war in Iraq. Even so, in Iraq itself and in the wider region across the Middle East it had far less impact. This was mainly because knowledge of prisoner abuse was already widespread, either through the regional media or through the experiences of individual prisoners released from detention. Abu Ghraib just provided some confirmation of what was already assumed to be widespread abuse.

As far as the insurgency itself was concerned, it was evolving into a dispersed phenomenon:

> The government faces an insurgency estimated at between 20,000 and 50,000 strong. These fighters are organised in as many as 70 cells, operating largely independently and at best with attenuated coordination. With no coherent centre of gravity and with no overall leadership, the insurgency cannot be defeated simply by the application of brute force.[4]

In this context, perhaps the most indicative comment was that made by Donald Rumsfeld in June 2005:

> This insurgency is going to be defeated not by the coalition – it's going to be defeated by the Iraqi security forces, and that is going to happen as the Iraq people begin to believe that they've got a future in that country.[5]

This represented a radically different assumption to that prevalent at the start of the war in March 2003 when it was confidently expected that US and coalition forces would easily control any opposition and Iraq would make a rapid transition to a stable American ally.

In November 2004, George W. Bush was re-elected for a second term in the White House, winning with a clear majority. This enabled the administration to say that it now had a clear mandate for its policy on the war on terror, including the termination of the Saddam Hussein regime and the subsequent occupation of Iraq, in spite of the continuing problems. On the basis of the election result, it might have been expected that the administration would have demonstrated considerable confidence in its policies, especially the likelihood that the Iraq insurgency would be defeated. In practice the failure of the Fallujah assault to have any discernible effect on the insurgency did much to reduce that post-election optimism, so that by April 2005, prospects for stability in Iraq appeared to be very limited indeed.

The Wider War

Although most attention in the United States was focused on Iraq, there were substantial security problems developing in Afghanistan. By April 2005, US ground forces were experiencing considerable overstretch because of the combined commitments in Iraq and Afghanistan, and there was a strong desire on the part of Washington to persuade NATO allies to back an expansion of the ISAF resources, possibly enabling the United States to draw down some of its troop commitments in the country. By the early summer of 2005, there were indications of a Taliban revival, made more likely because of the persistent failure of the Pakistani armed forces to take firm control of districts bordering Afghanistan, especially North and South Waziristan.

Furthermore, the wider al-Qaida movement remained active including an attack on the Australian Embassy in Djakarta in September 2004 and the bombing of the Taba Hilton in Sinai the following month. It was not therefore possible to claim that Afghanistan was being restored to peace, nor that the al-Qaida movement was in retreat, nor that the Iraq insurgency was in decline. Thus by May 2005, the Iraq War was entering its third year and the conflict and instability in Afghanistan was heading towards a fifth year since the 9/11 attacks and the subsequent termination of the Taliban regime. In such a context, the next year might indicate whether existing policies might succeed, whether they might be maintained with little success or whether there might just possibly be an examination of the policies themselves. These issues are explored in the following twelve chapters covering the months from May 2005 to April 2006, with a concluding chapter relating the developments to longer-term trends.

2
US Options in Iraq – May 2005

At the end of April, the security situation in Iraq looked particularly bleak. There had been a lull in insurgent activity at the time of the elections at the end of January and in the weeks that followed, but it came back with renewed effect by early March and the violence was maintained in April. The situation was made worse by a political stalemate lasting three months that prevented the formation of a full cabinet in the new Iraqi administration. Given that this interim government was only due to hold power until the end of the year, and was expected to formulate a new constitution by August, the prognosis for a stable political settlement involving Sunni politicians as well as Kurds and the majority Shi'a was poor.

Even so, there appeared to be a possibility that the announcement of a cabinet at the end of April might have a positive effect and, to some analysts, May was therefore seen to be a pivotal month. If there were to be a decrease in the level of insurgent activity, stemming perhaps from a loss of community support, then there would be some reason for longer-term optimism. This would be in marked contrast to the impasse that had developed in Iraq.

In the event, there was an opposite effect; the weight of evidence indicated that the insurgency was actually gaining in strength. During May, the US death toll, at 80,[1] was the highest for five months, and the loss of life among Iraqis was massively higher, with at least 500 people killed.[2] The US casualties also included over 550 wounded, with about half of them serious injuries. Given that US forces were progressively concentrating on the training of Iraqi police and army units, and were less heavily involved in patrol activities, this level of casualties was causing particular concern.

One development towards the end of the month was the increasing prominence of a point of view, both from senior military in Iraq and by US political figures, that the insurgency would not be defeated by coalition forces but only by Iraqi security forces supported by an Iraqi nation that needed to become increasingly opposed to the insurgents. This change of outlook contrasted markedly with the views that were common in US quarters in the first two years of the war. While acknowledging the problems, there was almost always an unwritten assumption that coalition forces, dominated by the exceptionally well-equipped US armed troops, would eventually be able to control and defeat the insurgents. This new orientation was effectively an admission that the insurgency would not be countered by military means alone. Even so, it was also acknowledged that Iraqi security forces would require some years of training to bring them to the point where they could exert control.

At the same time, it was also clear that there would be a substantial and permanent US presence at perhaps four major military bases, even if it did eventually prove possible to reduce the occupying forces.[3] The question of permanent bases first surfaced in a *New York Times* report shortly after the termination of the Saddam Hussein regime in April 2003. There had been little further information available, apart from some data on major construction projects at several bases, but further reports in the US press during May appeared to confirm the validity of the original story.

Given the difficult situation facing US and other coalition forces in Iraq, it is appropriate to consider the possible options from the point of view of the Bush administration. There are essentially four possibilities for the United States – defeat of the insurgency, redeployment of US forces in Iraq, a US defeat and withdrawal, or a long-term conflict with an uncertain outcome.

1. Insurgents Defeated

The insurgency is brought fully under control within a year or so, by a combination of US military capabilities and the rapid development of the Iraqi security forces, and a government is in place in Baghdad that is supportive of the United States.

If this was to happen, then the situation within two to three years might involve US forces numbering barely 20,000 in the country as a whole, located in a few major bases that might primarily be adjacent to Baghdad and the major oil fields. Together with substantial forces in neighbouring Kuwait, the United States would have the means to support a client government in Baghdad should it face renewed security problems at a later date. Indeed, in view of the possibility of a later upsurge, the Iraqi government could be more or less guaranteed to be cooperative with Washington since its survival could well depend on the future availability of US military power. While such an outcome would be immensely attractive to the Bush administration, given the current circumstances, all the indications are that there is little prospect of this.

Furthermore, such an outcome could have long-term consequences for the United States. It would necessarily involve a substantial US military presence measured in decades rather than years, helping to maintain the security of Iraqi oil supplies and exerting a wider influence in the Persian Gulf. This might even ensure an amenable Iran, one that would be unlikely to cause any instability in the face of US military success and the indirect control of a client government in Baghdad. In practice, even in this 'ideal' outcome, there are two related issues. One is that the very presence of such large US forces in Iraq would be likely to prove a magnet for the wider movement of Islamic paramilitaries, whether linked directly to the al-Qaida movement or not. Furthermore, such paramilitary groups are not operating on a week-to-week or month-to-month timescale, but see their confrontation with foreign occupying forces and local elite regimes as measured in decades. A US military presence operating over a similar timescale would stimulate radical paramilitary responses for as long as it was there.

2. Redeployment of US Forces in Iraq

A second outcome could be the maintenance of a substantial US military force at the designated permanent bases in Iraq but also in a number of other bases away from the major centres of population.

Such a situation might involve 60–80,000 US troops – a large number but markedly less than the 150,000 currently in Iraq, and therefore reducing the current problems of overstretch that are affecting the US Army in particular. Furthermore, such a force would be very much a back-up force to Iraqi government units. It would have essentially disengaged from the urban areas and would therefore be less prone to casualties, even if there were occasions when it had to provide military back-up for the Iraqi government. If such support was primarily a matter of air power, then the consequences in terms of casualties could be even lower. Moreover, a much-diminished presence of US forces in urban areas might eventually limit the extent of anti-Americanism, even among the Sunni communities.

Such an outcome would depend on the extent to which Iraqi government forces could control the towns and cities of Iraq, but, if this proved very difficult, it would be an outcome that would still involve far fewer problems for the United States military than the current insurgency. It would be a crude calculation – and could even be a matter of letting the urban areas of Iraq take care of themselves, while securing the strategic oil fields and their export routes, working in particular with the Kurdish communities in the north-east of the country.

Such a development is, to an extent, in line with what is known about the plans for the permanent military bases.[4] There is likely to be one base relatively close to Baghdad, perhaps 40 miles away. This could serve as a support base for the government of the day, but would still be well away from any major urban area to limit attacks on the base by insurgents. Two other bases are expected to be located in the northern and southern oil fields, with the northern base perhaps on the fringe of Kurdish-controlled territory and the southern base close to the major oil fields but also near enough to Basra, Umm Qasr and the oil export terminals on the Persian Gulf. The fourth base is likely to be in western Iraq, quite close to the Syrian border but also in the region of the western desert that may have substantial oil deposits still to be proved.

This second outcome depends on a rapid degree of success in training Iraqi security forces, or else an acceptance that the United States can serve its principal interest of securing Iraqi oil reserves while allowing the cities to be in a near permanent state of unrest and insurgency.[5] It would be an uncomfortable solution but might be more realistic than any thought of fully controlling the insurgency.

Where it would most likely prove unworkable is that substantial military forces would be required to secure the oil supply routes, the insurgency might evolve in a form that could not be limited by the use of air power, and there might even be a violent change of regime, bringing to power neo-Ba'athists or another deeply anti-American regime. In such circumstances, a further effort at regime termination might be required, with all the military and civilian consequences that this might entail. Even if there was not such a regime change, there is no guarantee of a diminishing insurgency, and the sizeable US presence in Iraq would still act as a magnet for the broader regional groupings of Islamic paramilitaries. From their perspective, it would still be seen as a neo-Christian occupation, in alliance with Zionist Israel, that was seeking long-term control of Arab oil.

3. US Withdrawal

The third option is consequent on a complete change of policy in Washington involving an acceptance that the Iraq operation is a disaster and that the only option is a rapid US withdrawal, even before Iraqi security forces can be expected to maintain control.

Whatever the eventual outcome in Iraq, be that a civil war or even the rapid emergence of a neo-Ba'athist regime, such a withdrawal would at least bring to an end the continuing loss of life and injuries among US forces and the growing domestic antagonism to the Iraq War.

Such a change of policy is unlikely but not impossible. One of the developments in recent months has been the change in the public mood in the United States, with a marked decline in support for the war in Iraq. Even with George W. Bush's re-election only seven months ago, there has been a substantial shift in public opinion in two respects. One is that there is growing opposition to the war itself and the other is that a large proportion of Americans does not feel that the Iraq policy is making the United States any safer.

Although the ongoing violence in Iraq hardly features on the network news channels unless there is a particularly major incident, the effect of the sheer numbers of casualties is becoming much more prominent across the country in a quite different way. With 1,700 troops killed and many thousands evacuated back to the United States with long-term and often severe disabilities, this is bringing home to people the costs of the war on a township or city district basis. More than 10,000 families and far larger numbers of friends and more distant relatives have been directly affected by the war in this manner, and while their predicaments and frequent unhappiness are not addressed in the national media, they are picked up by local newspapers and radio and TV stations. The end result is a growing awareness, at community level, of the human costs of the war to the US armed forces. This is coming at a time when some of the leading independent analysts and some senior military are questioning the US military posture in Iraq, even to the extent of querying its long-term viability.

It would be quite wrong to claim that this amounts to sufficient political pressure to result in a real change in policy, but it is certainly the case that a further increase in the intensity of the insurgency could make this a central issue in the second George W. Bush administration. Against this, though, are the consequences of a precipitate withdrawal from Iraq. Were this to happen, and given the central importance of the security of Persian Gulf oil reserves, the United States would be facing its biggest foreign policy reversal in decades. Withdrawal from Iraq would cripple its entire policy for ensuring Gulf security and would have much wider implications for the whole idea of a New American Century. In such a context, the idea of a rapid withdrawal is highly unlikely unless there was to be a calamitous increase in US casualties in Iraq.

4. Endless Insurgency

The final possibility is that the current insurgency lasts indefinitely, becoming something of a stalemate between weak Iraqi security forces that cannot maintain the security of the state on their own, backed by the US military presence, and insurgents who cannot develop sufficient strength to threaten the Iraqi government or cause an American withdrawal.

Such a situation could last for several years but might ultimately lead to some kind of compromise in which a majority of the supporters of the insurgency were brought into the political process sufficiently to undermine the insurgency itself. While this is certainly possible, it would involve some years of war, with the huge human costs that this would involve, and even such an eventual compromise is by no means certain.

While most analysis of the Iraq War concentrates on the insurgency as a domestic matter, it also has to be seen in its wider context. Over the past two years, Iraq has become a magnet for radical Islamic paramilitaries, giving a substantial boost for recruitment into movements such as al-Qaida and providing a basis for a region-wide growth in anti-Americanism. Even if the insurgency within Iraq was eventually to diminish, with some degree of political compromise achieved, a fundamental aspect of US policy will still be the maintenance of permanent bases in the context of that essential feature of US policy in the Middle East, ensuring the security of Gulf oil reserves.

Prospects

Given current circumstances it is highly unlikely that the insurgency can be defeated within the next two to three years. Nor is it likely that there will be a fundamental change of policy by the Bush administration leading to an early withdrawal of all US forces from Iraq. What is more probable is the continuing of the insurgency, with neither of the opponents able to achieve their aims. It is certainly possible that this might eventually lead to the second of the outcomes discussed here – the effective abandonment of the cities by the United States and a retreat to the margins, given that those 'margins' include the major oil fields.

What does have to be recognised, and is almost always ignored in current analyses of the conflict, is the underlying significance of the region's immense oil reserves – two-thirds of the world's total supplies and vital not just to the United

States, Europe and Japan, but increasingly to China and India
as well. This is the main reason why the United States will
not leave Iraq, whatever the difficulties it faces, and it is for
this reason that we face the prospect of decades, not years,
of conflict.

3
Iraq, Afghanistan and US Public Opinion – June 2005

A Long or Short War?

During June, the insurgency in Iraq persisted at the intense level of the previous month, with numerous attacks on the Iraqi police and security forces, further bombings of oil facilities and a number of assassinations.[1] Several hundred civilians were killed during the course of the month, and the US forces had 78 people killed and well over 400 wounded.

Against this background, and in the early part of the month, there were remarkably conflicting statements from senior members of the Bush administration about the likely development of the war. The Vice-President, Dick Cheney, expressed the view that the insurgency was in its last throes, a view that has been expressed many times over the past two years by others in the administration, yet still unusual since it came at a time of particularly intense insurgent activity.

Very shortly after Mr Cheney's comments, the Secretary of Defense, Donald Rumsfeld, took a very different view, suggesting that insurgencies such as that in Iraq could take as long as ten or twelve years to overcome.[2] His opinion was even more significant in the light of comments he had made a short while earlier, where he said that the insurgency could not be defeated by US forces but had to have an essentially internal

solution, with Iraqi forces eventually taking the main responsibility for security. Although an apparently straightforward
comment, the implications of this statement are considerable,
especially in the context of the many occasions since April
2003 where US military officials have expressed confidence in
a near-term victory.[3]

The implication of Mr Rumsfeld's view is that the substantial
US military forces, numbering close to 200,000 if one includes
support forces in neighbouring Kuwait and air and naval units
elsewhere in the region, are not able to defeat an insurgency
numbering a core of perhaps 20,000 activists. Bearing in mind
that the United States military has by far the best equipment
in the world, including a huge range of satellite, airborne and
ground-based intelligence and reconnaissance systems, such a
view being expressed by the US defence leadership is remarkable
in its own right. Taken together with Mr Rumsfeld's subsequent
comments about a ten–to-twelve-year insurgency, a picture
emerges which is in keeping with the previously-expressed
views of a handful of independent analysts in the United States
and Western Europe, but these have been views which have
been almost entirely ignored, if not derided, until now.

Mr Rumsfeld's opinions caused immediate consternation,
especially when placed alongside those of Mr Cheney.
Subsequent statements from the Vice-President's Office
suggested that 'last throes' could imply a period of continued
violence, and Mr Rumsfeld's comments about a long war were
immediately countered by a statement from the new Prime
Minister of Iraq, Mr Jaafari, that he expected security to be
greatly improved within two years.

The levels of violence in Iraq during the course of June
certainly indicated a robust insurgency deeply rooted in a
support base which stretched across a significant minority of the
Iraqi population,[4] but there were two other developments during
the month that may together be more significant in determining
longer-term trends, not just in Iraq but concerning Mr Bush's

wider 'global war on terror'. One of these was a substantial swing in public opinion in the United States, moving quite markedly away from support for the war, and the other was a further upsurge in violence and insecurity in Afghanistan.

Afghanistan

In an earlier briefing in this series, the point was made that there were some signs of hope in Afghanistan, but this was in the context of major problems of opium production that had returned Afghanistan to its position as the world's leading supplier of illegal heroin. One of the reasons for a certain degree of optimism was that an anticipated Taliban revival the previous summer had not materialised, even though there were continual instances of violence.[5] In the past three months, much of the limited optimism has evaporated as the levels of violence have escalated. In April, in particular, there were several major incidents involving Taliban insurgents in conflict with soldiers of the 17,000-strong force that the United States is currently maintaining in the country. There were also a number of attacks on Afghan police units as well as assassinations of officials working for the Afghan government and for non-governmental organisations.

This pattern continued into May, and there were added anti-American tensions after *Newsweek* reported the apparent desecration of copies of the Koran at the detention centre at Guantanamo in Cuba. During June, actions by Taliban elements increased once more, and there were two particular factors that were indicative of the new capabilities of the Taliban. One was the marked tendency for guerrillas to act in much smaller groups than before and to operate more in urban environments, including the use of improvised explosive devices. There are indications that paramilitary groups from Afghanistan have been gaining experience in Iraq and then returning to Afghanistan. This is an extraordinary reversal of the trends that were more common in the 1990s, when it was Afghanistan that provided combat and guerrilla experience for paramilitary groups.[6]

The second factor was the ability of Taliban elements, on occasions, to operate in large numbers in defined environments. In the middle of June, for example, there was an exchange of fire between Taliban guerrillas and government units in the district headquarters town of Mian Nishin in Kandahar province that left nine Taliban dead. This was then followed by a much larger assault on the town that left it under the control of the Taliban for two days before they were repulsed, with substantial loss of life on both sides, by Afghan forces backed up by US air strikes.[7] Fighting then escalated elsewhere in Afghanistan, especially in Zabul province, with the United States bringing in helicopter gun-ships and A-10 ground attack aircraft supported by British Harrier aircraft. There was further heavy loss of life on both sides. Then, at the end of the month, US forces lost 18 people when a helicopter was shot down while trying to reinforce a Special Forces unit that had become isolated.[8]

US Domestic Opinion

Although there has therefore been a marked deterioration in the security environment in Afghanistan, this has only been a trend of the past three months or so, and there has been very little domestic reporting in the United States of the individual incidents except where there have been US military casualties. As a result, the extensive commitments of US forces to Afghanistan, the ongoing insurgency there, and the contrast with the original expectations of a peaceful transition, have had relatively little impact on US public opinion. What has been much more significant has been the impact of the widespread violence in Iraq, with a marked change in public opinion that has been surprisingly sudden.

President George W. Bush won a reasonably clear-cut victory when he sought re-election last November, and this was immediately taken as a firm mandate for his policies, including the 'war on terror' and the continuing occupation of Iraq. It has therefore been a surprise that public opinion has moved markedly away from the previous support for the Iraq War, and that this has been a sudden change, rather than a slow and progressive shift.

In a Gallup survey taken in June, nearly 60 per cent of respondents were in favour of a partial or complete withdrawal from Iraq, this being the highest figure since the war began well over two years ago. In another poll conducted for the *Washington Post* and *ABC News*, the proportion of those polled who believed that the Iraq War had not made the United States a safer place was above 50 per cent for the first time, and in the same poll, nearly 40 per cent said that the Iraq War was coming to resemble Vietnam.

The change in public mood has been paralleled by an increasingly difficult recruiting environment for the US armed forces, both for regular troops and for reserve forces.[9] The US Army, in particular, has had to put substantially greater resources into gaining recruits, including the deployment of many more recruiters, the investment in a large-scale television campaign and the provision of substantially increased cash bonuses to new personnel on enlistment.[10]

In spite of all of these inducements, the Army has persistently failed to meet its monthly recruitment targets, even when those targets have, on occasions, been lowered. The Army's May recruitment figures were actually some 35 per cent down on the original target figure, and Army National Guard enlistment was down by 29 per cent. Recruiting into the Marine Corps was less badly hit, as was recruitment for the Air Force and Navy, but the Marine Corps is relatively small compared with the Army, and regarded as more of an elite force, and the Air Force and Navy have suffered proportionally far fewer casualties in Iraq than the Army.

The change in public mood, and in recruitment patterns, is not easy to analyse given that the US national print and broadcast media have not provided coverage of the Iraq War that is anything like the intensity of the coverage in the latter part of Vietnam. There have been some exceptions, particularly among the East Coast broadsheets such as the *Washington Post* and the *New York Times*, but most of the broadcast media have given relatively little coverage and some, such as Fox News, have been unswervingly positive in their assessments.

Throughout the period of the war in Iraq, the Bush administration has been consistent in providing minimal official coverage for the return of those killed in action to the United States, and there has been a marked absence of senior administration officials being present at funerals or visiting the main receiving hospitals for casualties. In the ordinary way, this might have been expected to diminish the effect of casualties on public opinion, the more so as they represent a much smaller number than the losses in Vietnam.

Three factors appear to be making a difference, two of them affecting public opinion as a whole and the third having a greater effect on recruitment. The first factor is that while the loss of life is still under 2,000, there have been large numbers of serious injuries. The reason for this, as noted in earlier briefings in this series, is that a combination of body armour and very high levels of battlefield emergency medical treatment have meant that far more soldiers have survived, but have often done so with severe injuries including limb amputations and head, throat and groin injuries. Well over 10,000 troops have been evacuated from Iraq with combat injuries and an even larger number have returned to the United States with physical or mental illnesses or non-combat injuries.

The total number of people returning to the United States with serious injuries having potentially life-long effects is not available, but is now likely to be somewhere between 5,000 and 10,000. The effect of this, combined with over

1,700 deaths, is that communities across the United States are experiencing first hand the effects of the war, often with reports in local newspapers or local radio and television. Given that such media play a larger role in the United States than in most European countries, where national media have a greater impact, there appears to be a cumulative effect that is bringing home to people the costs of the war.

The second factor is that there are now some very competent analysts, some of them ex-military, who are casting doubt on the conduct of the war and are suggesting the need for new strategies. While such people have little impact outside of some broadsheets and National Public Radio, they are probably having an effect on opinion formers and some sectors of the legislature. It is noticeable that in the House, with its members serving two-year terms, there is a tendency to respond much more rapidly to changes in the public mood than in the Senate, with its six-year terms, and there have been recent examples in the House of bipartisan demands for the administration to consider an exit strategy from Iraq.

The final factor, relating to recruitment, takes us back to the issues of casualties. By and large, the US Army recruits from relatively poor communities, rather than from across all sectors of society. This has been a long-term trend and it means that in those districts that are more likely to provide recruits, there will already be many people serving in the Army. As a consequence, there is likely to be a greater knowledge of the level of casualties in Iraq because they disproportionately affect such communities. Such knowledge, and the hesitations about the war among those home on leave, combine to create a mood of greater resistance to recruitment, even if other job opportunities are poor.

While it is somewhat rash to suggest that the developments of the past few weeks are part of a long-term trend, since even Mr Rumsfeld himself is now talking of an insurgency lasting many years it is reasonable to suggest that views on the war among the population as a whole are unlikely to become more positive. That there has been such a change is shown by the decision of President Bush, at the end of June, to deliver an address to the nation on the need to stand firm. In that address, in front of a military audience, his main emphasis was on linking the Iraq War specifically to the more general 'war on terror' seeking to justify to his wider audience that the Iraq War was and is a response to the 9/11 attacks and therefore demands patriotic support. That such an address was thought necessary indicates the concerns in the administration over the change in the public mood.

Any Change in Sight?

Do these developments mean that any major change in the administration's policy in Iraq is likely in the short term? In terms of the options discussed in last month's briefing (victory, redeployment within Iraq, precipitate withdrawal, or a continuation of the current military posture), it is highly unlikely that there would be any immediate and wholesale withdrawal unless there was a massive further change in the public mood embracing intense opposition to the war. It is also highly unlikely that any kind of victory will be achieved over the insurgents during the life-time of the Bush administration. This leaves two choices, continuing with current policies or redeployment away from the cities, concentrating on the oil-production zones.

It is just possible that some degree of redeployment might now be considered, and it is even possible that such a redeployment might involve a new attempt to invite multinational forces into Iraq to play a more active role in internal security, perhaps even under a United Nations umbrella. This latter action, though, is unlikely, both from the perspective of the administration and its attitude to the United Nations, and the deep suspicion of most UN member states over the risks of an involvement in Iraq.

It is therefore reasonable to conclude that, in the near future, there will be no substantial change of policy, the war in Iraq will continue, as will the wider 'war on terror', including substantial military operations in Iraq. It also has to be recognised that if there was to be another major attack on US interests of the level of the 9/11 attacks, either in the United States or overseas, then the public mood would be likely to swing markedly in favour of the administration's current policies, with an intensification of both the war in Iraq and the wider conflict.

4
London, Sharm al-Sheikh and the al-Qaida Movement – July 2005

In the four-year period since the 9/11 attacks in New York and Washington, there have been numerous further attacks across the world. However we describe the al-Qaida group – as a network, a dispersed movement or almost a syndicate – it has been involved in orchestrating far more attacks than in the equivalent period before 9/11. These have included two double bombings in Istanbul and two attacks in Djakarta, attacks in Karachi and Islamabad and several in Saudi Arabia. There have also been bombings in Kenya, Morocco and Tunisia, the attack on the Sari nightclub in Bali, and attempted attacks in Rome, Paris and Singapore. The tempo of the attacks appeared to diminish after the multiple bombing of commuter trains in Madrid in March of last year, with a long pause of nine months following last October's attack on the Taba Hilton and a campsite in Sinai, both frequented by Israeli tourists.

During this nine-month period, there was a considerable increase in the number of suicide bombings in Iraq, and there has been a more recent upsurge in violence in Afghanistan, yet there was a view among some analysts that the al-Qaida phenomenon was beginning to run its course, at least as a globally active group. It was thought that a combination of an increasing concentration of jihadist paramilitaries in Iraq, combined with the killing or long-term detention of many al-Qaida operatives, meant that the risk of attacks elsewhere in the world was diminishing.

There were two parallel trends in this analysis that were not particularly complementary. One was that the overall problem of paramilitary action was likely to diminish because of the combination of attacks on the al-Qaida movement with the probability of containing and then defeating the insurgents in Iraq, including the foreign elements that had been drawn to the conflict. The other was that jihadist action was certainly being concentrated in Iraq but that it was far too early to say that the insurgency could be brought under control. On this more pessimistic assessment, if Iraq was to become a long-term focus for jihadist action it might even serve to revitalise the al-Qaida movement.

The overall view was still that the al-Qaida movement was diminishing in capability, and it is this view that has been hugely damaged by the major incidents in London and Sinai during the course of July. Moreover, this surge in activity has coincided with further problems in Iraq, so much so that any realistic analysis has to conclude that the global war on terror is not going as planned and that the al-Qaida phenomenon is still evolving, often in quite unexpected ways.

Sharm al-Sheikh

The attacks on two hotels and a market place in the Sinai resort of Sharm al-Sheikh on 23 July killed 88 people and injured over 200, even worse than the multiple bombings in Taba the previous October. There had been two much smaller attacks in Cairo in the intervening months, but there was a belief that the Mubarak government in Cairo had acted so forcefully against radical Islamist groups in Egypt in recent years that there was little risk of major attacks arising from domestic groups.

It is not at present clear whether the Sharm al-Sheikh attacks involved foreign elements, and there were initial reports that several people of Pakistani nationality had been detained shortly afterwards. Such an international connection was later denied by the Egyptian authorities and there were subsequent arrests of Egyptian nationals. If there was direct international involvement then this points to a loose al-Qaida connection, but if the origins were domestic, then it means that Egyptian government efforts at control have not been effective.

In any case, the al-Qaida organisation is now so diffuse that it appears to involve a multiplicity of groups with only the loosest of connections, so that a group of primarily domestic origins would see itself very much as part of a wider struggle, even if it directs its efforts at undermining what it sees as an unaccountable and elitist regime in Cairo.

The London Bombs

In London, four coordinated attacks on the transport system on 7 July left 56 people dead, including four bombers, and several hundred injured. Those responsible were all long-term residents in Britain, three of Pakistani origin from West Yorkshire and one Afro-Caribbean man who had lived most of the time in West Yorkshire. Two weeks later, there was an attempt at a further coordinated attack, but the four explosive devices failed to detonate. Twenty people were subsequently arrested, including three alleged bombers originating from the Horn of Africa, with a fourth person detained in Rome. Taken together, the London and Sharm al-Sheikh attacks suggest that al-Qaida and its associates retain a marked capability for actions across the world, a situation that largely counteracts the more positive assessment, from a western perspective, that was outlined earlier.

There are other features of the London attacks that are particularly worthy of note. The first is that there was no warning of the first attacks – indeed the level of security alert had recently been eased in Britain, even though the Group of Eight Summit at Gleneagles in Scotland was due to take place early in the month. While there had been periodic warnings of UK vulnerability, and possibly the detention of potential bombers the previous year, these particular attacks came out of the blue.

The second issue is that there is considerable evidence that the first group of bombers had set in motion their plan in conditions of considerable secrecy, so that even close family and friends were unaware of their intentions, even if some of them had become somewhat withdrawn from their previous social circles. The third is that there were at least two cells operating in Britain, with the second cell that undertook the failed attacks on 21 July having very little connection with the first.

The final issue is that determined efforts have been made across many of Britain's more multicultural cities to prevent a deterioration in community relations, but these have so far only been partially successful, with a marked increase in attacks on Islamic communities in the weeks following the attacks.

One focus in the wake of the attacks has been the determination of the UK government to separate out any perceived motive for the attacks arising from Britain's ongoing involvement with the United States in the occupation of Iraq.[1] Instead, the British government's representation of the attackers has been of nihilist groups that had little in the way of clear-cut aims and whose motivation had stemmed from a thoroughly warped and unrepresentative version of Islam, with no direct connection with Iraq. Determining whether this is a tenable position relates, in part, to the current state of the insurgency in Iraq.

The Iraq Insurgency

During the course of July, the insurgency in Iraq continued at an unrelieved intensity, especially in terms of attacks against Iraqi police and security forces but with hundreds of civilians being killed too. Iraq Body Count and Oxford Research Group, in a jointly-published report in the middle of July, estimated civilian casualties in Iraq at close to 25,000 in the first two years of the war, with over 40,000 injured.[2] In the compilation of these figures, now widely used across the world by policy makers and journalists, a careful and conservative methodology is used, so that the figures, while an accurate report of individuals killed and injured, probably underestimate the full toll.

Furthermore, Iraq Body Count has not attempted the almost impossible task of estimating the Iraqi military casualties in the three-week period immediately prior to regime termination in early April 2003. On the limited information available from coalition sources and some 'embedded' journalists, many thousands of conscripts and Republican Guard soldiers were killed then. If the reliable estimates for Iraqi civilian casualties are taken together with information on Iraqi military casualties and civil and military losses in Afghanistan, the global war on terror has so far cost 40–50,000 lives, about ten times the number of people killed so far by al-Qaida and its associates in the 9/11 attacks and the many other incidents since.

In Iraq, US military losses during July were lower than May and June but still higher than March or April, with 54 killed. In the five-week period from 30 June to 2 August, 579 US troops were wounded, 169 of them seriously. One of the most significant developments in the country has been the aftermath of the US assault on Fallujah last November. The city had previously been seen as a core location for the insurgents and not under Iraqi government or American control. It was therefore considered to be a substantial focus for insurgent action affecting much of central Iraq, so much so that US military commanders believed that it was essential to take control of the city, especially with national elections planned for last January. As a consequence, a major assault on the city was launched using considerable firepower, with the control of the whole urban area being achieved within two weeks.

The human costs were considerable, with perhaps a thousand people killed, many of them civilians, and the great majority of the 300,000 inhabitants fleeing the city as refugees. Around three-quarters of the housing stock was destroyed or damaged, as were most of the mosques, schools and public buildings.

Fallujah is relevant for two quite different reasons. The first is that the city is now under very tight security control, yet insurgents are still able to operate. Some 8,000 US Marines and Iraqi security personnel now control the city, supplementing a large Iraqi police presence, there is a nightly curfew and only six entry and exit points with long periods of waiting and personal searches. In spite of these security measures, insurgents within the city have been manufacturing car bombs and detonating them in the immediate area, including one that killed six US Marines. They have also firebombed two of the five new police forts constructed in the city, have narrowly missed killing the Iraqi special paramilitary force commander in the city, and have also caused several members of the new city council to resign their posts.

The implications for the wider insurgency are considerable. While it is the case that Fallujah was a key centre for the insurgency, the current level of security involving many thousands of US and Iraqi troops should be sufficient to maintain a very high level of control. That this has not proved possible demonstrates how deep-seated the insurgency is, as well as the extent of support for the insurgents.

The second reason for Fallujah's significance goes well beyond Iraq and takes us back to the wider global war on terror. One of the features of the current Iraq War is the presence of major news media that are not under the control of the coalition. These include the Al-Jazeera and Al-Arabiya satellite-based TV news channels that are watched by tens of millions of people across the region, as well as a number of mainstream web sites.

These sources provide 24-hour news coverage of what is happening in the country, with particular attention being paid to the civilian casualties. The events in Fallujah, in particular, have had a major impact across the Arab and wider Islamic world, with the 'city of mosques' acquiring an iconic status in terms of perceived foreign brutality. While the main satellite TV channels maintain relatively high standards of presentation and reporting there is, in addition, a very well-developed industry based on diverse groups producing videos, DVDs and web resources that are much more markedly propagandistic.

On their own, such items would have some effect in aiding support for the al-Qaida movement, but their effect is even greater when added to the very widespread availability of satellite TV news output. In one sense, the situation was made even more complicated by the western TV coverage of the Fallujah assault. At that time, the US military was convinced of the central importance of the city to the insurgency, and wanted to demonstrate the military capabilities of the US forces. As a consequence, TV reporters were embedded with troops and TV crews were able to get substantial footage of the assault from outside the city. Little was seen of the damage being caused by the aerial and artillery assault, but the footage of the munitions being directed towards the city from the perimeter was extraordinarily powerful. To an American TV audience it demonstrated the power available to the armed forces, suggesting that the insurgency could be controlled with little difficulty. To an Arab audience, on the other hand, it was little short of an outrage. Even many of the people across the region who had been adamantly opposed to Saddam Hussein's Ba'athist regime became increasingly and bitterly opposed to the US actions.

Al-Qaida and Iraq

The value of the coalition involvement in Iraq to the al-Qaida movement is difficult to judge, but there is copious evidence from opinion surveys that anti-Americanism has increased substantially across the Middle East since the war in Iraq began nearly two and a half years ago. In the immediate aftermath of the London bombings, there were many media interviews with people from Britain's Muslim communities and what was repeatedly forthcoming was a combination of views. There was persistent and trenchant condemnation of the London bombers and an abhorrence of what they had done, but there was also real anger expressed at events in Iraq. The loss of life in Iraq was not remotely used to justify the London attacks, but the impact of the destruction in Iraq was still evident.

For al-Qaida itself, Iraq has provided a substantial boost in support. It has been possible to represent the conflict as an American neo-Christian occupation of a key Arab state. In this view, Washington is engaged in an assault on Islam, aided by Zionist Israel, and is intent on maintaining control of the region's huge oil reserves. Recognising the propaganda value of this situation, al-Qaida associates have specifically linked Iraq to the wider war with the West, threatening continuing violence as long as the occupation continues.

In practice, the great majority of the insurgents in Iraq are from indigenous groups, including largely secular Ba'athists, but this is not of great concern to al-Qaida, as the movement may confidently expect the number of foreign recruits to the insurgency to grow substantially in the coming years. Moreover, there certainly are radical jihadists taking part in the insurgency, even if these are probably numbered in the very low thousands at present. One effect of their presence is that some of these young paramilitaries from other countries in the Middle East are spending time in Iraq with the insurgents, gaining first hand training and combat experience, and are then returning to their own countries. This is already a matter of substantial concern to the Saudi security authorities and there is also some evidence that some Afghan paramilitaries have gained combat experience in Iraq and are then taking that experience back to Afghanistan. This is a remarkable change, given that it was Afghanistan that was the combat training zone for al-Qaida a decade ago. Now it is Iraq, with the experience being carried back to Afghanistan.

Perhaps the most difficult issue to unravel is al-Qaida's longer-term aim in relation to Iraq. The direct influence of the movement in that country is currently minimal, but the wider value of the conflict is recognised and messages from the leadership now make this clear. Such messages talk of violence against coalition members continuing until the occupation of Iraq is ended, and this therefore consolidates George Bush's view that the Iraq conflict is part of the global war on terror.

Given Iraq's oil reserves, and the current establishment of several large US bases in the country, it is highly unlikely that the United States will want to withdraw from the country, and thereby forfeit influence, any time in the next decade, but this may well be exactly want the al-Qaida movement most wants. While calling resolutely for a coalition withdrawal, it is more likely that the movement would greatly prefer the insurgency to continue with at least the current intensity for as many years as possible. The reason for this is straightforward – the al-Qaida movement is engaged in a conflict intended to replace what it sees as corrupt, elitist and pro-western regimes in the Middle East with what it considers to be true Islamist rule, leading eventually to the creation of a region-wide Caliphate. This is not a process that is likely to be measured in years, but in decades, and an essential part of the struggle is recruiting far larger numbers of supporters.

Afghanistan had its value, not least in terms of training camps, even if much of the effort was directed towards supporting the Taliban in their civil war with the Northern Alliance. Iraq is becoming far more significant than Afghanistan to the achievement of al-Qaida's long-term aims. It has a fundamental resonance with the re-creation of an Islamic Caliphate, given that Baghdad was the seat of the most notable example, the

Abbasid Caliphate of over a thousand years ago.[3] Now under
western occupation, and already forming a rallying point for
supporters within the region, the natural extension of this is
to attract support from across the wider Islamic world.[4]

If the insurgency does continue for many years, then there
is ample opportunity for many thousands of young paramilitaries to work with the insurgents over the next decade or so,
coming to Iraq from across the world and getting training
and even direct combat experience. Moreover, Iraq is an even
more effective training environment than was Afghanistan
in the 1990s, since the conflict is primarily one of an urban
guerrilla insurgency involving many techniques of asymmetric
warfare. This is actually more relevant to future jihadist actions
than was Afghanistan, which involved much more in the way
of conventional military actions in rural and mountainous
regions, hardly similar to environments in London, Madrid,
Istanbul or Casablanca.

In short, al-Qaida sources may talk of the imperative of a
coalition withdrawal from Iraq, but it is highly unlikely that
this is what they wish to see happen. For them, Iraq becomes
not so much the immediate core focus of a war against western
forces and local elites, but much more of a means of developing
the paramilitary forces to enhance a decades-long conflict. In
this respect, Iraq really does have the potential to be a major
part of the global war on terror, but hardly in the way that
Mr Bush or Mr Blair might expect.

5
Gaza in Context – August 2005

During the course of August, Israeli settlers were withdrawn from Gaza and from some settlements in the northern part of the West Bank. Some analysts saw this as the start of a revitalised peace process, and it is certainly necessary to see this unusual development in its wider context. At the same time, the month of August also saw the aftermath of the London bombings, a continuing high-level insurgency in Iraq, further issues relating to Iran, and a significant attempt at an attack on two US warships at Aqaba in Jordan.

The Gaza Withdrawal

The withdrawal from numerous settlements in Gaza and from four small settlements in the West Bank was completed in an operation that was, from Mr Sharon's perspective, far less violent than had been expected. The numbers of settlers were small, around 8,000, but they occupied large areas of land and had been a continuing security headache for the Israeli defence forces, with those in Gaza living alongside well over a million Palestinians, many of them crowded into densely packed refugee camps. The withdrawal had some historical significance – it was the first of any substance since the evacuation of settlers from Sinai after the Camp David accords had been agreed between an earlier Likud leader, Menachem Begin, and Anwar Sadat of Egypt at the end of the 1970s.

The relative ease with which the operation was completed contrasted strongly with predictions of widespread violence and even armed resistance from the settlers, and there appear to have been three reasons for the rapid completion of the operation. One was that very large numbers of police and army personnel were used, around 30,000, and they received extensive training in order to handle the settlers with a minimum of violence, in marked contrast to tactics frequently used in dealing with Palestinians. A second reason was that a significant minority of the settlers were in Gaza for economic rather than religious motivations and were prepared to move when offered generous compensation.

The third reason was that in the balance between Israeli public support for the settlers and for the Israeli armed forces, it would be the armed forces that would win every time. While the withdrawal from Gaza caused considerable controversy in Israel, with the Jewish population divided over the issue, support for the armed forces is consistently at a high level, and this made it very difficult for the settlers to risk any kind of violent confrontation with the troops.

With the withdrawal completed, the issues that remain are the motivations for the policy and whether it marks a significant step on the path to a peaceful settlement. While Israel's dominant international supporter, the United States, has declared itself for an independent Palestinian state, with the Gaza withdrawal seen as a major step towards this, there appears to be no pressure being put on Israel to proceed with further withdrawals from the West Bank, occupied now for nearly 40 years.

Three separate motives lie behind the Gaza withdrawal. One is that the settlements were proving massively costly to maintain, given their encroachment into a heavily populated Palestinian territory. In this respect, it was not just the settlements themselves but the wide corridors needed for the routes in and out of Gaza and the large areas of cleared land that were required around each settlement. All needed constant round-the-clock guarding, and just for the benefit of a few thousand settlers.

A second motive is that an isolated Gaza presents much less of a security problem for Israel than one containing scattered settlements. All access from the sea is controlled by the Israeli Navy, the airport remains closed, the land border with Israel is heavily fortified and even the border with Egypt is controlled by the Israelis.[1] Moreover, the Gaza economy would be dependent on Israel for expansion, not least in terms of providing employment and markets, and even in terms of supplies of water.

A third motive is that the Jewish population of 'Greater Israel' – Israel and the Palestinian territories – is progressively losing the demographic war, in that, on current trends, Jews will be in a minority in the whole territory in perhaps a decade. This was an issue among Israeli politicians 15 or 20 years ago but was partly ameliorated, from their perspective, by the immigration into Israel in the early 1990s of around a million Jews from the Former Soviet Union and Eastern Europe. This altered the Jewish/Arab demographic balance for some years but the rate of immigration into Israel has now slowed to a trickle, while the Palestinian birth rate has been maintained at an unusually high level.

It is worth stressing that the high birth rate among Palestinians is not as a result of the kinds of factors that have operated in many third world states in the past five or six decades. Rather, it is a matter of direct intention for hundreds of thousands of Palestinians for whom raising large families is seen directly as part of their responsibility towards the future of their people. Indeed, this combines with the intractability of the peace process to result in a growing movement among some Palestinians and Israelis towards a 'one-state' solution, with all people in Israel and the occupied territories being full citizens with full voting rights. In such a future, and with

Israeli Arabs and Palestinians comprising about half of the total population, a secular state of some kind would be the likely outcome.

Such talk is anathema to most Jewish opinion as it would mark the end of the Jewish state and of wider Zionist aspirations, but it does indicate how deep-seated the issue of the demographic balance has become. Support for such a 'one-state' solution remains small, and comes mainly from Palestinians, but for many Zionists it is easy to see why it is seen almost as a time bomb striking at the very existence of Israel.

In these circumstances, withdrawal from Gaza removes well over a million Palestinians from this calculation, but it does not mean that an economically viable Palestinian state is made more likely. This depends on developments in the West Bank where all the indications are that the Sharon government has not the slightest of intentions of withdrawing – indeed consolidation is the order of the day. It is true that the four small and isolated settlements in the northern part of the West Bank have been evacuated, and it is possible that a handful more will be dismantled in the coming months. At the same time, though, three other processes are under way, all of which consolidate Israeli control of the great majority of the territory.

The first is that the building of the security barrier or 'wall' is continuing, especially through key areas around Jerusalem. This encroaches deeply into the West Bank in many places, effectively amounting to a land grab that creates 'facts on the ground'. Israelis argue strongly that this is an effective security measure against suicide bombers, but this would be more believable as a primary motive if the wall stuck to the old 'green line' that marks the Israel/West Bank boundary of pre-1967 days, instead of taking in large areas of Palestinian land.

The second process is the expansion of Israeli settlements in the West Bank, especially the building of large numbers of new settlements in Eastern Jerusalem and the surrounding countryside. Most such settlements are not occupied by religious groups but by young families that move in for economic motives because of the availability of subsidised housing. Even so, they steadily alter the geographical balance, making the idea of East Jerusalem as a future capital of an independent Palestine less and less feasible.

Finally, across the West Bank as a whole, many large Jewish settlements remain, all connected by strategic roads that divide the much larger areas of Palestinian population into numerous isolated cantonments that are easily controlled through scores of roadblocks. Transit between the north and south of the West Bank across greater Jerusalem is very difficult, but movement by Palestinians within smaller areas of the West Bank is frequently subject to long delays, consistently limiting the economic potential of the whole area.

Although these difficulties persist, the withdrawal from Gaza is still seen by many analysts as a substantial change for Palestinians, and it is just possible that extensive international support combined with restraint from Israel could see rapid social and economic progress, but this will depend on both internal and external politics. Of the former, although the withdrawal from Gaza has not been as divisive in Israel as was feared, it has caused very deep divisions within the ruling Likud Party, so much so that Mr Sharon now faces a leadership challenge from Mr Netanyahu who, if successful, would certainly harden his party's policies towards the West Bank.

Of the external political factors, most European states want to see further progress, including substantial withdrawals from the West Bank, but the mood in Washington remains firmly pro-Likud, backed by the influence of the Christian Zionists. The extent of this latter link is rarely appreciated, but it is not uncommon for evangelical Christian churches in the United States to be directly twinned with Zionist settlements in the occupied territories. This alone is a significant factor in

militating against a genuine long-term peace process leading
to a two-state solution.

Iran and its Nuclear Ambitions

One positive effect of the successful withdrawal from Gaza is
that it removes fears that a sudden Israeli air strike on Iranian
nuclear facilities might be engineered if there was a major
political crisis in Israel. Such a diversionary tactic may have
seemed implausible but was not ruled out in high political
circles in Western Europe. While the risk of such a strike from
Israel may have diminished, it has come at a time when the
new Iranian government under Mr Ahmadinejad has taken a
rather more robust line in its dealings with the EU3 (France,
Germany and the UK) over its putative nuclear ambitions.

This is also coincident with the formation of Mr Ahmadinejad's
new cabinet, drawn heavily from the Revolutionary Guard and
from senior intelligence figures, and representing a marked
departure from the government of his unsuccessful reformist
predecessor, Mr Khatami. At the same time, approval of the
new cabinet and of the more junior ministerial posts had to be
given by the Majlis (parliament) and this proved much more
difficult than expected, even though the Majlis currently has a
conservative majority. While most of the President's nominees
eventually got through, this unexpected problem indicates
that Mr Ahmadinejad is not a conventional conservative.
Much of his support stems from the Revolutionary Guard
and from those poorer sectors of Iranian society that have
become thoroughly disenchanted with the corruption and
incompetence that has been a feature both of reformist rule
and the clerical power base.

The significance of these issues for Iran's external relations,
especially on the nuclear issue, is far from clear. At the
technocratic level, Iran continues to develop its economic
ties with China, India and Russia, and there is certainly

widespread public support within the country for its nuclear power programme. It is probable that the current firmer stance with the Europeans will be at least maintained – Iran may not actively seek a confrontation with the United States, but also will not be inclined to change its policies in the face of US threats. In any case, developments in Iraq and in the United States itself have meant that the Bush administration currently has serious preoccupations of its own.

The Iraq Insurgency

Among these is the continuing insurgency in Iraq. August was one of the worst months for US forces since the war began two and a half years ago, with 85 troops killed.[2] Injuries also remained at a high level – in the four weeks to 30 August, 496 troops were injured of which over 150 were seriously injured.[3] Throughout the month, four issues dominated the overall picture. One was the large number of attacks on Iraqi security forces, continuing a pattern that had developed over the previous 18 months,[4] and the second was the persistent use of considerable force, including multiple air strikes, by US military units as they tried to take control of cities and towns in north-west Iraq.[5] Repeatedly it proved possible to clear insurgents out of particular districts, but they re-emerged almost as soon as the US forces were scaled down after the particular assault.

If the US aim has been to take control of districts and then hand them over to Iraqi security forces, then the policy is proving to be a consistent failure – the Iraqi forces do now have the capability to exercise control and the US forces are too thinly stretched to provide longer-term support.

The third issue was the continuing problem of economic sabotage by insurgents, with August seeing numerous attacks against the energy infrastructure. By the end of the month, fuel rationing seemed probable on top of immediate shortages, even though Iraq is one of the world's richest countries in terms of oil reserves.

The final issue was the continuing political stalemate as attempts were made throughout much of August to produce a constitution for submission first to the legislature and then to a countrywide referendum planned for October. While a constitution was eventually agreed, it currently does not have the support of most members of the Sunni minority and, as such, increases the longer-term risk of a decline into civil war.

Domestic Dissent

The continuing loss of life among the US military in Iraq, and the much larger numbers of soldiers being seriously injured are both having a cumulative effect on US public opinion. This came right to the fore during August when the mother of a soldier killed in Iraq, Cindy Sheehan, made camp close to George Bush's vacation ranch near Crawford, Texas, demanding an explanation from him for the Iraq policy. Her demonstration attracted widespread media attention and gave the first indication that a nation-wide anti-war movement might be starting.

At the same time, while President Bush's popularity has certainly slipped, there remains substantial support for the Iraq policy, even though the early response to the devastation left by Hurricane Katrina in New Orleans and along the Gulf Coast contrasted markedly with US rapid reaction capabilities when applied to Iraq. Opponents of the war remain hopeful that there has been a change in the domestic mood, but, as suggested in previous briefings, the oil security factor remains central to the thinking of the Bush administration and it would take a fundamental long-term change in domestic politics to have any substantial effect on the US military posture in Iraq.

Al-Qaida

Although there were suggestions that the perpetrators of the bombings in London may have had links with the wider al-Qaida movement there was little evidence of this until right at the end of the month when a pre-recorded videotape of one of the bombers was broadcast on the Al-Jazeera satellite news channel, along with that of one of the al-Qaida strategists, Ayman al-Zawahiri. This does not confirm a connection, as the videotape may have been acquired by other means than a pre-planned operation, but it indicates the links that exist.[6]

In any case, although the London bombings indicate a continuing capability for action by militants against US allies, an incident with even greater implications may well turn out to be the attempted attack on two US warships in the Jordanian port of Aqaba on 19 August. A 40,000 ton amphibious warfare ship, the USS *Kearsarge*, and a second ship, the 15,000 ton USS *Ashland* were targeted by three Katyusha unguided artillery rockets that had been secreted into the town. All three missiles missed their targets, with one killing a Jordanian guard at a nearby warehouse and another landing across the nearby border in Israel.

This was the first major attack on US Navy ships since the bombing of the USS *Cole* in Aden Harbour in 2000, but its significance also lies in the location of the attack. Jordan is a particularly close ally of the United States in the region and there had been a widespread view that its security forces had a very strong control of dissidents and potential militants. The 19 August attack, which was quickly claimed by the Iraq-based al-Qaida associate, Abu Musab al-Zarqawi, indicates that this is not the case, and that the al-Qaida movement has capabilities that stretch across the region.

Conclusion

While it would be good to be able to suggest with confidence that the Israeli withdrawal from Gaza might prove to be

a turning point in the Israel/Palestine peace process, and
that the loss of domestic support for the Bush administration might cause a reformulation of policy towards the Iraq
insurgency, there is little to support either proposition. The
Gaza withdrawal could still be the start of something much
more positive but there has been no substantive change in the
US position on Israeli activities in the West Bank.

Perhaps more troubling is the fact that the UK government,
at least at the level of the Prime Minister, is simply not prepared
to countenance any possibility of a connection between the
London bombings and the situation in Iraq. Until that outlook
changes, it is difficult to see the UK embracing a realistic
assessment of the current state of President Bush's global war
on terror.

6
The US Military and the 'War on Terror' – September 2005

Overstretch

One of the issues that has been in the background for the past two years has been the extent to which the United States armed forces are capable of maintaining their current level of military activity as the core actors in President Bush's global 'war on terror'. There have been numerous reports of problems with recruitment as well as resentment by National Guard and reserve units having to spend far more time on deployment than had been expected. Furthermore, the 2006 defence budget has had to be adjusted to put more emphasis on the Army and less on new high-tech weapons.

At first sight it may be difficult to see why there is this problem of 'overstretch' – at the present time, the United States is maintaining around 200,000 members of its armed forces in Iraq, Kuwait and surrounding countries, but this is small compared with close to 400,000 troops that were used in the 1991 war to evict the Iraqi forces from Kuwait. Why, then, is there a problem? Essentially it stems from a combination of circumstances, some operational, some historical and some relating to a contradiction between the kinds of wars the United States is fighting and those that its political and military planners were expecting to fight.

On the operational side, the key issue is that Iraq and Afghanistan are turning out to be long wars that are mainly involving just two of the four branches of the US armed forces, the Army and the Marine Corps. Neither the Navy nor the Air Force is greatly involved in either country, except for the air transport units of the Air Force which are certainly under some strain. The US could field twice as many troops in the 1991 war against Iraq, but that did not involve long-term deployments, with the need to rotate units at six-to-twelve-month intervals for year after year. If the 1991 war had evolved into a much longer occupation in the face of insurgent forces, similar problems would have emerged, even though the US armed forces were then substantially larger.

Cold War Legacies

This brings us to the second issue – the historical context. During the latter years of the Cold War, the United States maintained powerful military forces based on a volunteer system. The draft (conscription) was very much a thing of the past, but the requirements of the Cold War confrontation with the Soviet Union meant that the Army, Air Force, Navy and Marine Corps were all well-funded, with defence budgets exceeding $400 billion a year (at current prices). One major component of the armed forces was a heavy presence in Western Europe, including tens of thousands of Army personnel in West Germany, complete with thousands of main battle tanks, armoured personnel carriers and self-propelled artillery.

After the end of the Cold War and throughout much of the 1990s there were subtle changes in the armed forces that collectively amounted to a major re-orientation of their capabilities. On the nuclear side, most of the tactical nuclear weapons were withdrawn from deployment, and the size of the strategic nuclear forces was scaled down. In parallel with this change, two other aspects of the Cold War forces were substantially altered. One was the massive US Navy emphasis on anti-submarine warfare and the other was the Army's concentration of troops and heavy armour in Western Europe. Both of these were cut back drastically, with the US Navy losing any possibility of getting near the '600-ship Navy' that had been the aim of navy planners in the 1980s. In practice, though, it was the Army that took the heaviest cuts, especially in terms of personnel, whereas the Navy got off relatively lightly and the US Marine Corps was hardly affected by the changing climate.

The thinking behind this was that very large land forces were no longer appropriate for the post-Cold War era. We were now moving into what some naval analysts were calling the era of the 'violent peace'. There was no longer a massive enemy in the form of the Soviet Union, but there would be many diverse threats to US interests around the world. President Clinton's first Director of the CIA, James Woolsey, had put it succinctly at Congressional hearings in 1994 when he said that the United States had slain the dragon but now lived in a jungle full of poisonous snakes. George W. Bush was to put it in his inimitable style during the 2000 election campaign when commenting on the changes since the Cold War era: '...it was a dangerous world and we knew exactly who the "they" were. It was us versus them and we knew exactly who them was. Today we're not so sure who the "they" are, but we know they're there.'

During the 1990s, the Army took the brunt of the cuts in terms of personnel, although its rapid deployment units such as the 82nd Airborne Division were maintained and there was an increased emphasis on Special Forces. Some key components of the Navy were also maintained, especially the carrier battle groups. These were seen as massive mobile air bases that could be deployed to regions of crisis and potential threat. Six carrier battle groups had been used in the 1991 war against Iraq, and this demonstrated powerfully to the military planners that the US Navy had a major role to play in keeping the violent peace.

The US Air Force lost many of its European and East Asian deployment centres because of the collapse of the Soviet threat. Many bases in Germany and the UK were closed down, and even the important Clark Field base in the Philippines was evacuated. At the same time, though, the Air Force argued strongly for its capability to reach any part of the world in a matter of hours, contrasting this with the weeks that it could take to deploy a carrier battle group. It did not win the day, with the Navy keeping almost all of its carriers, and this aspect of inter-service rivalry continues to the present time. Even so, the Air Force did well enough to enable it to maintain powerful forces, especially with an emphasis on the 'air expeditionary wings', essentially self-contained air groups that could be deployed to pre-prepared bases overseas, especially in the Middle East, when required.

The most interesting case was the US Marine Corps. During the Cold War, US Marines numbered close to 200,000, substantially larger than the entire British Army, with numerous large amphibious warfare ships, logistics support ships and their own air force centred on the AV8B, a version of the British Harrier jump-jet. After the Cold War, the Corps was maintained at close to its peak levels of the 1980s, primarily because this was exactly the kind of force that could play a role in responding to regional crises.

Military Forces for a New World Disorder

What this all meant was that the US armed forces as a whole had been progressively reconfigured to fit the perceived demands of an unstable world. The US Air Force now placed much more emphasis on global reach, the Navy relied more heavily on its aircraft carrier battle groups and the Marine Corps was ready and willing to make substantial if short-term deployments in time of crisis. The US Army had taken the biggest cuts, but could at least field some sizeable forces for rapid deployment and also had a back-up system of reserves and National Guard units in an emergency. What it had lost, though, was its Cold War capability to maintain large forces in overseas deployments for long periods of time.

These moves towards short-term interventionism as the key to US military posture got a further boost in 2001 when the George W. Bush administration came into office, and Donald Rumsfeld took up the post of Secretary of Defense. While Rumsfeld recognised the need to have the Marine Corps and the Army's rapid deployment units, he believed even more forcefully in rapid intervention, primarily using air power. He did not see any real likelihood of large ground forces being necessary in the foreseeable future and envisaged an even leaner high-tech US military as the key force in ensuring the security of the New American Century.

The combination of the new thinking and the facts of military dispositions goes a long way to explaining why there was an implicit belief that the termination of the Saddam Hussein regime could be achieved primarily through intensive air strikes and the rapid movement of Army and Marine Corps units into Iraq. It is worth recalling that there were analysts at the US Army War College who were suggesting, in the run-up to the war, that such forces might not be sufficient, and it was the Army Chief of Staff, General Eric Shinseki, who said, in February 2003, that it would take several hundred thousand troops to secure Iraq after regime termination. Shinseki was sharply criticised by Rumsfeld's then deputy, Paul Wolfowitz.

A Dose of Reality

The apparently easy termination of the Taliban regime in the last three months of 2001 seemed to support the ideas of Rumsfeld and others. Heavy air bombardment, the careful use of Special Forces and the boosting of local surrogates in the form of the Northern Alliance all seemed to demonstrate that the 'new thinking' about American military power was along the right lines. Four years later it looks very different, and there is a certain irony in that it is the issue of Afghanistan that has recently demonstrated the problems now being faced by the US military, especially the Army.

Although the Taliban regime was terminated with ease, many of the militia simply melted away back to their towns and villages, or to neighbouring Pakistan. From both sides of the border they have re-emerged to fight a bitter guerrilla offensive that has proved to be an unexpected and unwelcome development for the Pentagon. The Bush administration had originally expected to be able to scale down its forces in Afghanistan to the point where it was maintaining two large air bases, at Bagram near Kabul and at Kandahar, together with a number of smaller units elsewhere in the country. Most of the personnel would be from the Air Force, there would be little need for frontline troops and Afghanistan could be secured with a sympathetic regime in power in Kabul.

Instead, the Taliban's guerrilla campaign continues in the south and east of the country, currently tying down around 20,000 troops, with 17,000 of them from the United States and others from Britain, Australia and a handful of other coalition partners. The bitter war continues with no respite – 51 Americans and as many as 1,000 Afghans have been killed so far this year, most of the latter being civilians – and there is no end in sight.[1] With the United States committed to maintaining much larger forces in Iraq, there is now an urgent need to try and scale down the Afghan commitment.[2]

Assistance from NATO?

To try and achieve this, Donald Rumsfeld went to Germany during September to try and convince NATO defence ministers to increase NATO's contribution. At present, NATO leads the International Security Assistance Force (ISAF) in Afghanistan, around 12,000 troops stationed mainly in Kabul and some other cities away from the key areas of the insurgency. As the name suggests, ISAF is a peace-enforcing operation and has been fairly successful in this role. Rumsfeld was hoping to see this force amalgamated with the larger combat forces operating elsewhere in Afghanistan under US leadership, the effect being to bring in some of the most experienced of the combat troops available within NATO's European partners, and thereby easing the pressure on the US forces.

Rumsfeld's efforts to achieve this came to nothing, with at least five NATO countries – Germany, France, Spain, Turkey and the Netherlands – all against the proposal. It is possible that Britain may offer more in the way of combat troops if it can extricate itself from its heavy commitments in Iraq, but that is currently the most that the United States can expect. For the time being, at least, the Pentagon will have to keep its forces in Afghanistan while it tries to control the insurgency in Iraq, all the while trying to maintain the required levels of recruitment into the Army at a time when this has proved very difficult. Even with greater monetary bonuses and a lowering of entry standards, the US Army failed this year to meet its recruitment targets.

An Unexpected World

Four years into George Bush's global 'war on terror' and two and a half years into the occupation of Iraq, it is all turning out very differently to the notion of versatile high-tech forces maintaining US security interests across the world. The continuing conflict in Afghanistan may not be large scale, and there may be no more than a few thousand Taliban and other militia active at any one time, yet they are tying down 20,000 troops. In Iraq, most estimates of the size of the active insurgency speak of around 30,000 people involved. They are requiring over 160,000 US and other troops in the country itself, with tens of thousands in Kuwait, Qatar and other western Gulf states. Moreover, this is clearly long-term, yet it would be hugely controversial if the Bush administration were to seek to re-introduce the draft. Some tentative steps have been taken to make it possible to call up some groups of specialists, but even this is likely to incite opposition if they are implemented.

What the United States is facing in Iraq and Afghanistan is an entrenched form of asymmetric warfare in which determined paramilitaries have sufficient support from their own communities and are fighting on their own territory. With all its reconnaissance and surveillance systems and with all its firepower and communications assets the Pentagon is simply not able to gain the advantage and therefore faces major long-term commitments that are as unexpected as they are difficult to maintain.[3]

One of the main effects of this predicament is a pronounced tendency to use those military capabilities in which the United States has an overwhelming advantage, and these frequently come down to firepower. Moreover, with US casualty figures in Iraq now approaching 2,000 dead and over 10,000 seriously injured, there is a very strong tendency to use firepower on a massive scale, whether it be artillery, helicopter gun-ships or strike aircraft.[4]

This has been seen repeatedly over the past two years, most notably in Fallujah last November, but is continuing on a near-daily basis. For much of the latter part of September, for example, US forces were engaged in a large-scale programme of assaults against towns and villages in north-western Iraq towards the Syrian border. Scores of people were killed, many of them civilians, and thousands of buildings were damaged or destroyed. The aim was to prevent insurgents using the region for links with Syria and for mounting attacks elsewhere in Iraq, but almost all the experience of similar operations in the past shows that the insurgents themselves, unlike many of the civilians, manage to get advanced warning of the US military operations and simply melt away until the US forces have moved on to other places.

The net effect of all of this is that substantial military operations are having, as their major effect, an increase in the hostility of many Sunni Iraqis to the US occupation. What this means is that the United States is not just finding itself with very large forces pinned down in a long-term military occupation in a manner that was wholly unexpected barely four years ago, but its chosen response – the frequent use of its firepower advantage – is proving persistently counterproductive. That is a measure of the predicament that the United States now finds itself in as it persists with its chosen means of fighting President Bush's global 'war on terror'.[5]

7
Iraq in a Wider Perspective –
October 2005

The month of September had been considered a relatively easy month for US forces in Iraq, in that only 49 American military personnel were killed. This was the lowest figure for six months and was one of the factors that gave rise to another phase of the oft-repeated claim that the insurgency was easing. In some ways, even this 'good news' was misleading, in that the military deaths in September were still higher than for any of the six months from May to October 2003 when the insurgency was getting into its stride.

In any case, the optimism was short-lived in that the following month, October, turned out to be one of the worst since the start of the war, with 96 troops killed. Apart from the two months of intensive fighting around Fallujah in April and November of last year, there was only one month since the war started, January of this year, when the death toll among American forces was higher. Overall, the period from August to October 2005 has been particularly difficult for the US forces in Iraq. It is not just the death toll, standing at 230 for the three months, but it is also the persistently high rate of injuries. In this period, 1,700 US personnel have been injured, with 600 of them sustaining serious injuries, most of these being evacuated to Landstuhl military hospital in Germany and then on to the United States for longer-term treatment. About half of all the troops sent back to the United States are eventually discharged from the armed forces, many of them disabled for life.

There had been an expectation that there would be a surge in the violence around the time of the referendum, but this had also been anticipated during earlier elections, and maintaining US troops and Iraqi security forces on high alert had actually reduced the incidence of attacks on previous occasions. While the referendum did yield a positive result for the new constitution, it came close to falling as two provinces rejected it. Since three were required to do so for it to fail to be approved, the constitution goes ahead, but it seems likely to do little to curb the insurgency.

Meanwhile, the casualties among Iraqi police and security forces continue at a high level. Iraq Body Count now reports up to 30,000 casualties since the war began. While the great majority have been civilians, the police and security forces continue to be severely affected. There have also been some highly sophisticated attacks, including one on the Palestine Hotel in Baghdad that is used widely by the foreign media. The hotel is across the river from the heavily protected 'green zone' that houses the Iraqi government, US Embassy and many other US facilities, but the Palestine Hotel is in a heavily protected compound. On 24 October, two bombs were used to breach the outer protected perimeter around the hotel complex, and a cement truck loaded with explosives was then rammed through the damaged perimeter and into the compound before exploding. Although the hotel was not destroyed, at least 17 people were killed.[1]

Countering the Insurgency

Two trends have recently emerged in the evolution of the insurgency. One is the increased use of large improvised explosive devices against road convoys including the more regular use of shaped charge explosives that are able to pierce

armoured vehicles.[2] Many of the recent American casualties
have been caused by such IEDs and they are also being used
against British forces in the south-east of the country, so
much so that the British Army is making far more use of its
limited force of helicopters in order to move troops around
and minimise road patrols.

One of the responses on the US side is to increase the number
of major military operations in the towns and cities north-
west of Baghdad towards the Syrian border. This region has
been presumed to be both a centre of insurgency and a route
for foreign paramilitaries coming in from Syria. There were
several occasions in October when combined US/Iraqi forces of
well over a thousand troops were deployed against particular
centres of population. A feature of these attacks was the use
of substantial firepower, including helicopter gun-ships and
strike aircraft. This often involved the targeting of presumed
insurgent strongholds with substantial bombing raids, leading
to reports from US sources of many insurgents killed. All too
often, however, these were followed by reports from local
hospitals of large numbers of civilian casualties.[3] Although it
is difficult to be sure, it is probably the case that as the deaths
and injuries among US troops stay at a high level, and as the
US military forces appear unable to curb the insurgency, so
there is a marked tendency to play to their strengths. The main
one is the immense firepower advantage, but the two inevitable
results of this, as seen in Fallujah a year ago, are firstly the
civilian deaths and other collateral damage, and secondly the
persistent reporting of these actions across the region, even
though they may seldom reach into the western media.

Al-Qaida Evolving

Chapter 4 sought to analyse the significance of Iraq for al-
Qaida. In a general sense it is certainly the case that the
continuing western occupation of Iraq is very useful to the

al-Qaida movement. Since one of the long-term aims of the movement is to establish a renewed Islamic Caliphate, the fact that Baghdad was the main city of the Abbasid Caliphate for several hundred years is a powerful motivating force. The occupation of Iraq can readily be presented as a neo-Christian endeavour involving Israeli (Zionist) cooperation that is an affront to Islam and is, furthermore, also motivated by a determination to control Arab oil.

Moreover, the high civilian death toll in Iraq, and the widespread reporting by regional satellite news channels of the death and destruction wrought by high-tech US weapons systems both serve to increase anti-Americanism, not just in the region itself but also across the wider world. This may not all be directly relevant to al-Qaida, given that foreign paramilitaries still make up only a small minority of the insurgents in Iraq, but this is likely to grow with time, and it is certainly the case that Iraq is becoming significant as a combat training zone for young Islamic paramilitaries.

In the past four years, al-Qaida has lost a number of its key leaders, either killed or detained, and has also lost its main base in Afghanistan. As such it is limited to those parts of Pakistan and Afghanistan that are not under government or US control. Many analysts argue that this is not a major problem for the movement since it has undergone a metamorphosis into a much more dispersed entity. Having lost its more structured organisation of pre-9/11 days, al-Qaida is now more of an idea than a firm movement, and is therefore much more difficult to infiltrate, track and counter.

Such a form of analysis also points to the many different attacks that al-Qaida and its affiliates have carried out in the past four years, including Bali, London, Djakarta, Istanbul, Karachi, Casablanca, Madrid and many more. This list excludes a number of attacks that may have been countered by western agencies, including potential incidents in Rome, Paris and Singapore, a cluster of incidents that was augmented by George Bush in October to include planned attacks in Los Angeles, London's Heathrow Airport and the Straits of Hormuz in the Persian Gulf.[4]

In listing these further operations, President Bush was seeking to show that al-Qaida is being curtailed and that the United States and its coalition partners are having successes in his global war on terror. It can also be interpreted in a rather different way. If this 'weakened' organisation is able to mount all the attacks listed above, while having other operations intercepted, it suggests a capability that is formidable, and is certainly much greater than its level of operations in an equivalent period before the 9/11 attacks.[5]

There is, though, a further factor to consider. An objective assessment is that the al-Qaida movement remains active, and is capable of encouraging if not actually directly organising attacks across the world. Moreover, it can do this when it has only the loosest of structures and operates without a coherent base. While this could be represented as a successful transformation, not least because it makes counter-terrorism operations so difficult, it could also be said to be a disadvantage in that an even greater capability could result from a combination of this dispersed movement with a more coherent base that would demonstrate that the movement actually holds distinct territory. If this combination was to evolve, then the wider jihadist movement, with al-Qaida at its centre, could become very much more potent.

Al-Qaida in Afghanistan and Pakistan

Could such a combination evolve? There are two current possibilities – Afghanistan and Iraq. In Afghanistan, the Taliban insurgency continues, currently tying down around 20,000 foreign troops, mostly American. This force operates in those eastern and southern provinces of Afghanistan in which Taliban and other guerrilla groups are currently operating. It is distinct from the International Security Assistance Force (ISAF) that engages in peace-keeping and peace-enforcing operations in Kabul and some other cities. At the present time, the guerrilla forces may have influence over some districts but cannot be said to control them in the manner in which the Taliban regime did in the 1990s.

Nor is it possible for al-Qaida militias to operate freely in North and South Waziristan and other districts across the Pakistan border. Osama bin Laden and other elements of the surviving leadership, together with paramilitary support, may be able to move around in the Afghanistan/Pakistan border zone, but that is different from having a degree of territorial control that enables them to maintain training camps and other facilities. This is what was in existence prior to the termination of the Taliban regime at the end of 2001. It is true that many of the jihadists who went to the training camps in Afghanistan during this earlier era were actually doing so in order to join the Taliban in their ongoing civil war with the Northern Alliance. This was a more significant role for the training camps than preparing paramilitaries for action in other parts of the world, although that may have been a subsidiary function.

At the present time, it is unlikely that Taliban or al-Qaida militia have adequate territorial control in Afghanistan to establish training camps, and they certainly do not have such capabilities in Pakistan. At the same time, relatively small groups of insurgents are tying down close to 20,000 western combat troops supported by helicopters, strike aircraft and a wide range of space-based and land/air-based reconnaissance facilities. Their very ability to do so means that such insurgents are continually getting combat training. For the US forces, with their problems of overstretch, Afghanistan is becoming a costly diversion while they have much larger forces committed in Iraq. Their predicament is that they cannot withdraw, nor can they hand over to less well-equipped forces from coalition partners, because of the risk that Taliban/al-Qaida paramili-

taries could make territorial advances that could give them the
potential to re-establish bases.

A New Base for Al-Qaida

If this is a potential problem in Afghanistan, then it is a far
greater risk in Iraq, even if the number of foreign paramilitaries
remains relatively small so far. The insurgency shows no signs
of diminishing, but regional geopolitics, especially the security
of Gulf oil supplies, means that there is no serious prospect
of the United States withdrawing substantially from Iraq. As
argued in Chapter 2, one option for the United States forces
would be what is sometimes called 'Plan B', a withdrawal from
the cities and consolidation of US troops in a small number
of large heavily protected bases, including some strategically
located close to the major oil fields.[6]

Such a redeployment would leave US forces far less vulnerable
to insurgent attacks but would enable them to aid a client
government in Baghdad when necessary. It was pointed out,
though, that this would depend on the successful training and
operation of Iraqi police and security force units, with them
taking over many security functions still being undertaken by
US forces. So far this has had made little progress. Moreover,
there would still be a major US presence in Iraq, serving as
a continuing magnet for young paramilitaries drawn to Iraq
from throughout the region and beyond.

Even so, a withdrawal from the cities and a much greater
reliance on air power to limit insurgents and support a client
government would have the domestic political advantage of
decreasing American casualties. Given the current unpopularity
of the Bush administration, there is a real concern in Republican
Party circles that the mid-term congressional elections in a
year's time could see major gains for the Democrats. If they
were to achieve substantive majorities in the House and Senate,
as is certainly possible, the last two years of the Bush admin-

istration could make for a seriously 'lame duck' presidency, limiting the chances for a conservative victory in the 2008 Presidential election.

For these reasons of domestic reality, some version of 'Plan B' might well come to the fore in the next four to six months, but this may now have the added drawback of allowing the al-Qaida movement to gain a much stronger base within Iraq. This is by no means certain – the al-Qaida presence in Iraq makes up a small minority of the insurgency, even if its leadership is both innovative in its methods and particularly skilled at publicising its actions. In spite of this, there are persistent tensions between foreign jihadists linked to al-Qaida and what might best be described as neo-Ba'athist and Iraqi nationalist insurgents.

The real issue is one of timescales. If the US forces do progressively withdraw to major bases while supporting the Iraqi government and retaining large forces in the country, they are likely to be entrenched in such dispositions for some years to come. With continuing violence and the consequent civilian casualties, Iraq will remain a magnet for paramilitaries from many other countries, providing a combat training zone that may have an effect stretching over more than a decade, not least as an increasing proportion of the insurgents come from abroad.[7]

This was already recognised as one of the consequences of the occupation of the country. What is new is the idea that the US predicament may go further than this if Iraq ends up having substantial districts that are simply not under any kind of central control. In these circumstances, not only will the country constitute a long-term training environment in urban guerrilla warfare, but it will also be available as a base for al-Qaida operations. As Afghanistan was in the 1990s, so Iraq may be in the coming decade – that is the extraordinary potential consequence of the decision to terminate the Saddam Hussein regime by force.

8
The Politics of War –
November 2005

In the period from June to September, domestic opinion in the United States began to shift towards opposition to the Iraq War to an extent that had not been apparent in the previous two years. This was partly due to the steady stream of casualties, both those killed and the many thousands seriously injured. Although the federal government did much to avoid publicity for these losses, the local media across the United States did report the deaths or serious injuries, often at neighbourhood or district level. With some 10,000 people killed or maimed, this meant that there was a growing awareness of the human costs of the war.

The impact of the casualties was also publicised by the actions of Cindy Sheehan, who had lost a son killed in Iraq, when she camped near President Bush's ranch in Crawford, Texas for much of August. She became a focus in an unexpected manner, providing the domestic media with a means of relating to the unease that had been developing across the country for several months. Other factors indirectly affecting the Bush administration were its failures over the effects of Hurricane Katrina, and also a perception that the frequent expressions of optimism over the progress of the Iraq War were simply not being borne out in practice. By November, the political climate in the United States was changing quite markedly.

This raises the question of whether there will now be a major change of policy over Iraq and this, in turn, relates to events both in Iraq and Jordan.

The Insurgency

The months of October and November were amongst the worst for US casualties since the war began, apart from April and November 2004 when the two assaults in Fallujah proved particularly costly. In these two most recent months, 180 US troops were killed and over 1,000 injured, with over 400 of them sustaining serious injuries. This was in spite of the fact that US forces were engaged in a number of high profile attacks on insurgents in which helicopter gun-ships and strike aircraft were used repeatedly to take advantage of the overwhelming firepower that the United States could bring to bear. The insurgency, meanwhile, continued without a pause in other parts of the country, with a series of brutal yet effective suicide attacks, frequently made against Iraqi police and security force units.

One of the most striking examples of the capabilities of the insurgents came at the end of November. For much of the month, US forces had mounted a series of major military operations against presumed rebel centres in western Iraq, towards the Syrian border. They were being conducted on the basis that these towns and villages were both the centres for insurgent support and also served as crucial transit routes for jihadists entering Iraq from elsewhere in the region through Syria.

One particular operation involved 2,000 US Marines and 500 Iraqi troops in action in the town of Hit. While that operation was actually under way, a force of several hundred heavily armed insurgents attacked US bases and Iraqi government offices in the nearby regional administrative centre of Ramadi, a previous focus of US military operations. The insurgents then proceeded to take over areas around the city centre, setting up roadblocks and patrolling the streets. It was a symbolic gesture in that they only maintained this stance for a few hours, melting away into the neighbourhoods immediately afterwards. There were no deaths and few injuries and the US military could claim that it was no more than a gesture. In one sense it was, but that misses the point – in the midst of a nearby US operation, the insurgents were able to put together a force of hundreds of militia, take over the centre of a city and then disappear.

This follows a pattern that has been repeated on numerous occasions across western and central Iraq over the past 18 months. It was particularly noticeable at the time of the all-out assault on Fallujah a year ago, which was followed almost immediately by a partial takeover of the city of Mosul by insurgents.

One of the recent responses of the US forces to this problem has been to combine operations against insurgent centres with subsequent garrisoning of 'cleared' areas by US and Iraqi forces. The problem here is that this either depends on a plentiful supply of US forces, which is proving difficult to maintain, or else on the reliability of the Iraqi forces. The latter remains questionable, in spite of repeated US claims that the training programmes are proving effective. In many parts of Iraq, police units in particular are proving to be inextricably mixed up with militias to the extent that they are not operating under central government control.

Since many Iraqi security units are effectively operating as Shi'a or Kurdish peshmerga units, their opposition to Sunni insurgents and, more importantly, the communities from which they come, exacerbates the targeting of these units by insurgents. During the course of November, much more information came to light over the operation of detention centres, the practice of torture and the use of death squads against presumed supporters of the insurgency. While this in no way downplays the often brutal actions of the insurgents, it does mean that the possibilities of undercutting the motivations of the insurgents are minimal.

A related issue has been the repeated tendency of the US authorities in Iraq to represent the insurgency as increasingly a matter of external jihadists dominating the actions, with the Jordanian paramilitary leader, al-Zarqawi, being a central figure. This has a particular value in domestic politics in that Zarqawi can be described as the al-Qaida leader in Iraq, so countering the insurgency therefore becomes central to President Bush's global war on terror, a point made forcibly in recent speeches by Vice-President Dick Cheney.

The concern with one individual has been an enduring feature of the war on terror since the 9/11 attacks, with Osama bin Laden and Mullah Omar being early examples. In practice, there have been few sightings of Zarqawi in recent months, and little indication that he is in any way central to the insurgency. His group may have a singular ability when it comes to publicising their actions, but they are unlikely to be significant in overall terms. One of the markers for this assessment is that of the tens of thousands of suspected insurgents taken into custody in the past two years, only 5–10 per cent have been from outside Iraq, and in recent US sweeps through towns and cities in western Iraq, the proportion has been ever lower. The reality is that the insurgency remains an essentially Iraqi phenomenon.

Even so, it is certainly likely that Iraq will become steadily more important to the wider al-Qaida movement in two respects. One is the continuing coverage of civilian casualties and collateral damage on Al-Jazeera and other news channels, backed up by much more propagandistic videos, DVDs and web-based material distributed across the world. The other is the steadily increasing importance of Iraq as a jihadist training zone.

Further indications of this are that young paramilitaries from Afghanistan now travel to Iraq where they are able to spend several months in training camps that have been established, not least in the vicinity of Fallujah in spite of the heavy US presence in the area. They may become involved in the insurgency but, more importantly, they are given direct tuition in the construction and use of a range of improvised explosive devices including remote-controlled detonation systems. This knowledge is then taken back to Afghanistan.[1]

This phenomenon is still small-scale and is certainly not at the level where, as Washington argues, foreign jihadists are dominating the insurgency. Instead, it is more of a marker for the future, providing the al-Qaida movement with a capability that may have a considerable long-term value. One of the ironies of the current situation is that such jihadist training potential is useful to the al-Qaida movement that sees its conflict with the United States and its coalition partners as stretching over some decades. It follows that it would be best for the movement if the US occupation of Iraq lasted for many years. That is in contrast to the outlook of most of the Iraqi insurgents, where the motivation is much more one of wanting an immediate US withdrawal. Within that contradiction could lie a future conflict of interest between the Iraqi insurgents and foreign jihadists, but there is little evidence of that at present.

Jordan

If the complex insurgency in Iraq is a major problem for the US forces in that country, the multiple bombings of the Grand Hyatt, Radisson and Days Inn hotels in Amman on 9 November was a reminder of the capabilities of the wider paramilitary movement. Back in August there had been an unsuccessful attack on two US warships in Aqaba harbour. This had caused some consternation in US military circles as the Jordanian government was thought to have had a firm control of radical Islamist movements in the country, and the US Navy had assessed Aqaba as being a safe port for warships, even to the extent of renting warehouses in the port for storage purposes.[2]

The Amman bombings, which killed 57 people and injured scores more, showed that Jordan was even less secure than the Aqaba attack had indicated. Moreover, when these two attacks are put together with the bombing of hotels in Sinai, the attacks in the Balinese town of Kuta, the 7 July bombings in London and the attempted attacks two weeks later, and the bombing of a KFC outlet in a secure district in Karachi, this all suggests that the wider al-Qaida movement remains markedly active whatever claims the US authorities may make to the contrary.[3]

US Political Developments

Although the Amman hotel bombings were seen as significant in Washington, the main issue in the United States remains the persistent insurgency in Iraq and the rising number of US military casualties. What gave this a particular political relevance during November was the expressed view of one particular member of Congress that the US policy was deeply flawed and that withdrawal from Iraq should be actively considered. The problem for the Bush administration was that the politician concerned, John Murtha, could not easily be dismissed as an un-patriotic liberal. Murtha is a decorated Vietnam-era Marine who has served for three decades in Congress and has long been regarded as markedly pro-defence if not hawkish.[4]

Most other political figures can be dismissed, either by impugning their patriotism or by reminding them of previous congressional support for the war in terror in general and the termination of the Saddam Hussein regime in particular. This has not proved possible with Murtha, but the Bush adminis-

tration has chosen to respond by emphasising the essentiality
of victory in Iraq.[5] Among neo-conservative commentators
there has been a robust defence of current policies with the
criticisms, if there have been any, being along the lines that we
are not committing enough troops to Iraq.[6]

This is very much in the context of a war which is being won,
the consequence being that a pull-out now would be a case of
snatching defeat from the jaws of victory. It is an extraordinary
message, but one that is being repeated time and again, almost
now as a mantra from the right. The real question, though, is
whether this really is the strategy – to continue and perhaps
harden the military posture in Iraq in the expectation of victory
– or whether it is disguising a rethink of policy.

The answer to this core question is frankly uncertain at
present, but it is probable that some changes are now being
entertained although these will fall far short of a precipitate
withdrawal from Iraq. What is particularly important to the
Bush administration is to avoid sufficient unpopularity from the
Iraq War to cause a Republican loss of control of one or both
houses on Congress in the mid-term elections in a year's time. If
that were to happen, it would seriously damage the Republican
chances of holding on to the White House in 2008.

This domestic political necessity, coupled with the prevailing
problems in Iraq, may well mean that the so-called 'Plan B'
in Iraq (option 2 of the possibilities discussed in Chapter 2),
may be implemented over the next six to nine months. This
would involve the consolidation of US forces in a number of
secure bases, the withdrawal of perhaps 30,000 troops ahead
of the mid-term elections next November, and greater efforts
to train Iraqi police and security forces. There would be a
particular emphasis on helicopter-borne forces, both gun-ships
and troop carriers, to back up Iraqi forces when they face the
insurgents, but there would also be a marked decrease in the
numbers of US ground troops and, just possibly, a consequent
reduction in casualties.

Coupled with the tacit acceptance of the power of Shi'a and Kurdish militias to oppose Sunni insurgents, the presence of US-backed Iraqi government forces able to rely on massive US airborne firepower would be sufficient to maintain a semblance of order until after the elections. It would also mean that any Iraqi government, of whatever political complexion, would be reliant on US forces in order to be able to remain in power. It would therefore be under very heavy US influence, making it to all intents and purposes a client regime.

From the standpoint of the Bush administration this would be a messy and incomplete outcome but would be substantially better than the predicament currently being experienced in Iraq. There is no guarantee that it would bring greater stability in the longer term – the use of airpower might in due course incite an insurgent response involving portable anti-aircraft missiles on a much larger scale than at present, and the maintenance of large US bases, however well protected, will serve as a continuing focus for the domestic insurgency, as well as being a long-term cause for the wider al-Qaida movement.

From the Washington standpoint it fulfils two requirements. One is that it may produce slightly more satisfactory circumstances for the domestic political context in the run-up to next November's elections, and the other is that the United States still retains a powerful influence in Iraq which, given the oil and gas reserves of the region, remains utterly essential.[7]

At the same time, even to think in these terms is a cause for reflection on how things have changed compared with the expectations of nearly three years ago. Then, rapid regime change followed by a client regime, a small number of US bases and a clear demonstration to Iran of US intentions and capabilities were all seen as the foundations for the Greater Middle East Initiative, producing regimes across the region that were essentially the allies of the United States. In some circles that may remain the dream but it is certainly not even remotely the reality, either now or in the near-term future. That, though, is overshadowed by next November's elections, and we are likely to see the US military posture in Iraq increasingly dominated by domestic political realities. That is the direction in which the politics of the war is now taking us.

9
Control Without the Consequences – December 2005

In political terms, the early part of December seemed to be proving one of the more positive periods for the Bush administration in relation to Iraq. Following several months of increasing opposition in the United States, President Bush and senior administration officials went on the domestic offensive with a series of speeches stressing the progress being made in Iraq. This coincided with two developments within that country – the election of a new administration and polling evidence that a majority of Iraqis were optimistic about prospects for the country.

The elections passed relatively peacefully, not because of increased counter-insurgency activity by the US forces but because the majority of the insurgents within Sunni communities were prepared to allow the elections to take place to ensure a larger Sunni impact on the outcome. The end result was uncertain and it may take months to see a stable administration set up, but it did make for a period of relative calm.

Shortly before the election, the BBC published an opinion poll undertaken by Oxford Research International showing a fair degree of optimism among the 1,700 Iraqis polled across the country. Sixty-one per cent thought the government had done a good or very good job, with only 33 per cent holding contrary views. Furthermore, 64 per cent of those polled thought things would get better during 2006. At the same time, their priorities for the coming year would be improved internal security followed by withdrawal of foreign troops. Furthermore, there were sharp regional variations, with more optimism in the Kurdish north and the Shi'a south and much greater pessimism in central Iraq where the insurgency is concentrated.

This polling evidence, coupled with the successful holding of the elections, was used powerfully by the Bush administration during its December offensive, promoting the idea that Iraq had 'turned the corner'.[1] Such an optimistic assessment has many parallels from the past three years of the war. They have included expectations on many occasions that particular events would seriously limit if not cripple the insurgency. Examples were the killing of Uday and Qusay Hussein in July 2003, the capture of Saddam Hussein himself five months later and the anticipated effects of several sets of elections. Even the assault on Fallujah in November 2004 was expected to hugely damage the insurgency, as that city was seen as its epicentre.[2]

Regrettably, by the end of December the pattern of previous examples of short-lived progress had been repeated, with a swathe of insurgent attacks on US forces, Iraqi police and security personnel and on civilians. The greatest intensity of suffering was experienced by ordinary Iraqis, but December was another difficult month for the Americans, with 68 killed and over 400 injured. The two weeks of the Christmas/New Year period, in particular, were expected to be quiet, but in that period alone US forces had 174 people injured.[3]

Attacking the Iraqi Economy

In addition to the continuing intensity of attacks on security forces and civilians, one other feature of the insurgency that has come to the fore has been an escalation in the attacks on the country's economic infrastructure, especially its oil industry. Before the war, the Saddam Hussein regime was able to maintain oil exports at a rate of around 2 million barrels per day (bpd), sometimes reaching 2.5 million bpd. This was at a time of a tough sanctions regime and may have been only half of Iraq's potential export capability at that time. After the termination of the regime, the oil export levels never regained even the previous levels reached under sanctions, but did get as high as 1.8 million bpd around the start of 2005. The rest of 2005 saw a pronounced decline and in December oil exports fell to just 1.1 million bpd, the lowest level since exports resumed a few months after regime termination in April 2003.

If it were not for the continual acts of sabotage, Iraq could probably export nearly three times the current level, around 3 million bpd, and serious investment in new facilities could double this. The reality, though, is that insurgents have become increasingly skilled at disrupting supplies, sometimes being so effective at blowing up pipelines and destroying road tankers that whole refineries have had to be closed down for lack of supply outlets.

An End to Funding?

The effect within Iraq is that serious fuel shortages persist, there is disruption to electricity power generation and the revenue required to redevelop the crippled economic infrastructure is simply not there. Moreover, this predicament comes at a time when the United States has decided to cease its own funding for reconstruction. Of the $18.4 billion so far committed about half has had to be spent on security or has been lost as a result of insurgent attacks, and the Bush administration has now decided not to seek any more funding from Congress in the coming financial year. The expectation is that Iraq will have to find its own resources or aid will have to be provided by other countries.

This change in policy is paralleled by a similar if smaller-scale move in Afghanistan, where the 2005 USAID budget for Afghanistan, about $1 billion, will reduce by 40 per cent in the next year. This is part of a more general move by the United States to cede much of its military posture to its NATO allies. The US will still maintain considerable influence in Afghanistan, not least through a sustained if diminished military presence at the two big air bases at Bagram and Kandahar, but it will seek to do so with fewer commitments and a decreased risk of military casualties.[4]

Back in Iraq, the decrease in funding support is being accompanied by a distinct change in the military posture. It became clear during December that one other military change that had started to become evident earlier in the year, was progressing rapidly. This is a substantial increase in the use of air power against the insurgents.

Until August 2005, the number of air strikes conducted against presumed insurgent targets was averaging around 25 a month. By November it had escalated to 120 and was expected to reach 150 in December.

In the past, air strikes have employed large bombs – 1,000 lb or 2,000 lb devices – but satellite-guided 500 lb bombs have become the norm, the expectation being that these would be less destructive in urban areas, avoiding excessive collateral damage. This trend is expected to continue as the first of a new consignment of 3,000 new 250 lb bombs become available. While the sheer level of damage inflicted may diminish, the manner in which insurgents are so closely intermingled with civilians in dense urban neighbourhoods means that avoiding civilian casualties is frankly impossible. Moreover, as the US Air Force and the US Navy intensify the use of strike aircraft in counter-insurgency, so the civilian casualties are likely to increase.

An Evolving Strategy

What emerges from all of this is an evolving strategy that seeks to maintain control but without the complications stemming from insurgencies in both countries that have proved so difficult to control. In Afghanistan, for example, the termination of the Taliban regime was expected to cripple the al-Qaida movement, make the Taliban militias irrelevant and allow the country to develop as a client state of Washington, with a couple of US bases to ensure security. Instead, 19,000 troops are tied down in an enduring insurgency that has seen an upsurge during 2005. The response from the Bush administration is to seek to hand over as much of the security work to NATO, with ISAF expanding into the south of the country, even if that means its being involved in counter-insurgency in addition to more traditional peace-enforcing and peace-keeping roles. The end result, from the perspective of the Bush administration, should be a reduced US military presence with no diminishing of Washington's influence over the political direction of the country.

In Iraq, it is even more blatant and is also geared very closely to the mid-sessional elections to the US Congress in November 2006. Not only will the United States rely more and more heavily on the use of air power against the insurgents, but there will be a substantial decrease in funding from Washington to support the reconstruction and redevelopment of the country. Whether that gap will be filled by other countries, by the World Bank or by revenues from oil exports is not clear, but none of these seems likely. No European country is prepared to provide aid at the huge level required, the World Bank would be deeply reluctant to be heavily involved in what remains a war zone, and there is little or no sign of an increase in oil revenues. Indeed, the consistent targeting of oil facilities makes this highly unlikely. It is more probable that Iraq will be allowed to stagger on, as long as US ground forces can begin to disengage from the insurgency and rely more heavily on air-power. In such a role they will continue to act as a guarantor of the survival of whatever government comes to power and, as such, that government will be indebted to Washington and will do its bidding as required.

This convoluted outcome, both in Afghanistan and Iraq, is currently the 'best-case' scenario for the Bush administration. If it works, then the otherwise adverse consequences for the mid-sessional elections might be minimised. Better still, a further decrease in US military exposure in both countries by late 2007 will help ensure a better prospect for a Republican candidate in the 2008 Presidential election.[5]

To repeat, though, this is strictly 'best case' from an American perspective, anything but 'best case' for ordinary people in both countries. It makes no allowance for a further upsurge in Taliban/al-Qaida activity in Afghanistan in the coming spring and summer, an upsurge that could put NATO's limited forces under huge strain and require US reinforcements. Nor does it allow for a persistent and evolving insurgency in Iraq that may make substantial troop withdrawals impossible. Most of all, it does not factor in the greater impact of the more extensive use of air power. The civilian casualties and physical collateral damage arising from this change of policy will be widely witnessed, thanks to the pervasive presence of media outlets such as Al-Jazeera. This will ensure that indirect US control in Iraq through the use of high levels of force will become even more effective in encouraging an embittered anti-Americanism, not just in the Middle East but in much of the majority world.

Overall, the twin wars in Iraq and Afghanistan are almost certainly still in their early stages. The Bush administration may seek a short-term improvement through these current changes in policy, but these very changes may actually ensure an increase in violence, quite possibly well before November 2008.

10
Iraq, Afghanistan and now Iran Once Again – January 2006

The evolving US policy in the 'war on terror' was analysed in the previous chapter and is readily summarised. Because of the changed mood in the United States in the past few months, it has become important for the Bush administration to adjust its military posture in both Iraq and Afghanistan. In the case of Iraq, it is desirable to be seen to be withdrawing some troops in the coming months, primarily because of the need to avoid the war being a damaging issue in the mid-sessional elections to Congress in November.

The troop withdrawals are likely to be scheduled for the summer months and may be fairly small-scale, perhaps limited to three combat brigades and their supporting elements, certainly less than a fifth of the US troops currently in Iraq.[1] Given the current level of the insurgency and the difficulties of replacing US troops with their Iraqi counterparts, this withdrawal will not be easy to engineer, and may be heavily dependent on the current moves to rely much more on air power in seeking to curb the insurgency. That this is likely to increase civilian casualties through 'collateral damage' may not be seen as an obstacle, even though it will further heighten the anti-American mood in Iraq and across the region.[2]

85

Afghanistan

In Afghanistan, where the insurgency is proving more deep-seated than had been anticipated, the US intention is to try and withdraw around 2,500 of the 19,000 troops currently in the country, with some of the burden being taken up by an increase in the size of NATO's International Security Assistance Force (ISAF), largely through a new deployment of British troops. ISAF's role has primarily been one of ensuring security through a peace-enforcement role, especially in Kabul and some of the larger towns and cities of the north and west of the country. The effect has been variable, but has rarely tipped over into embracing a counter-insurgency role.

That may change as the ISAF forces are deployed to new areas, especially those where they will replace US troops that have been very much involved in counter-insurgency actions. For the British armed forces, such involvement is not new – there have been units of UK Special Forces operating alongside US forces for many months, and there has also been a deployment of six Harrier strike aircraft. Even so, what is now envisaged as part of the ISAF expansion is substantial numbers of British troops directly involved in operations that are far more likely to include open combat with Taliban and other militias. This may have consequences for UK domestic politics as the controversy over UK involvement in Iraq is heightened by a new concern over activities in Afghanistan.

Moreover, this is coming at a time of two significant developments in Afghanistan, both of them indicating that the insurgency is becoming more deep-rooted. The first is that the current winter period has witnessed continued attacks on a range of targets, including US and ISAF forces, Afghan security personnel, government offices and officials and personnel working for aid organisations. All such groups have experienced such problems in the past but there has tended to be something of a pause during the more extreme winter months. This has simply not happened this year, suggesting that the Taliban and other militias are better organised and resourced.

This relates to the second issue, the decrease in Pakistani Army control of the border regions in Pakistan. In the past two years there have been a number of military operations in districts such as North and South Waziristan, with many of them proving costly to the Pakistani Army. In recent months there have been persistent reports that what little hold the Pakistani government had on such districts has largely melted away, leaving Taliban and other paramilitaries a considerable degree of freedom in which to train and collect supplies.[3]

That such a circumstance has evolved has been a real concern for the US military and specialist agencies such as the CIA, and one response has been to launch raids into the border areas of Pakistan from Afghanistan. In the early weeks of 2006, there were three raids, all of which were reported to have used Predator drones equipped with air-to-surface missiles. The most controversial was an attack on three houses in the village of Damadola, which was reported to be aimed at Ayman al-Zawahiri, the Egyptian-born associate of Osama bin Laden who is widely regarded as the key strategist for the al-Qaida movement. It later turned out that he was not present in the village at the time, but it is possible that three other senior al-Qaida members were present and were killed. What is certainly true is that a number of civilians were killed, most of them women and children.[4]

In all probability, the Musharraf government in Islamabad gave informal approval for this and other raids, but the public reaction was substantial, with large demonstrations in a number of towns and cities across the country.[5] This results in a severe dilemma for the Americans. In order to be able to withdraw troops from Afghanistan, they have to be as effective as they can in their own counter-insurgency activities, otherwise there will be a growing number of casualties among NATO's ISAF units, leading to considerable political controversy among

NATO's European member states, not least in the UK and
the Netherlands. But US operations are seriously limited by the
lack of Pakistani governmental control of the border regions,
hence the need for US forces to use armed drones to under-
take raids.[6]

To be able to do that, though, the American planners have
to factor in the likely effects of such actions on Pakistani
political stability. President Musharraf has already survived
several assassination attempts. He remains privately close to
the Americans but the more the US undertakes cross-border
actions, the more there will be a strong public reaction in
Pakistan. In the final analysis, though, US domestic politics,
and the need to withdraw troops, will take precedence over
any risks to Pakistani political stability. We should therefore
expect to see more cross-border activity, including air strikes
on presumed al-Qaida and Taliban units, in the coming
months, with the need to do so increasing as the spring and
summer approach.[7]

Over much of the period through December 2005 and
January 2006, western media attention tended to be focused
on the Iraqi elections and on the developing political and
diplomatic confrontation with Iran, with Afghanistan getting
far less prominent attention. It may be that the focus will shift
away from all of these towards Pakistan, for the first time in
several years.

Iran

What is well nigh certain is that the potential conflict over
Iran's nuclear ambitions will become much more prominent.
This has been a relatively low profile matter for much of the
last three years, mainly because of the US preoccupation
with issues in Iraq and Afghanistan, but also because of
European Union efforts to seek a diplomatic settlement and,
more recently, the Bush administration's concentration on the

aftermath of Hurricane Katrina. During the course of January, however, the issue rose rapidly up the political agenda and by the end of the month it was apparent that a full-scale crisis was in prospect.[8]

The consequences of military action against Iran, either by the United States or Israel, are analysed in a study from Oxford Research Group[9] and suggest some very problematic outcomes, including the potential for a protracted war. This makes it all the more strange that the mood has hardened, especially within the United States. In part, this is due to changes within Iran, but it also relates to the underlying reasons why Iran is such a particular concern for the Bush administration.

Within Iran, the election of Mahmoud Ahmadinejad last year was a surprise for most analysts. His principal opponent, Hashemi Rafsanjani, had the support of most elements of the theocracy that retains much of the power in Iran, but Mr Ahmadinejad was able to go over the heads of the current power base in Tehran, appealing directly to the poorer sectors of the electorate. He succeeded in part because of a widespread view among the electorate that much of the theocracy was distant and even corrupt, and also because of his own simple personal lifestyle contrasting markedly with theocratic opulence.

After coming to power he moved rapidly to consolidate his position, not least through major changes in Iran's diplomatic representation overseas together with replacement of many technocrats in ministerial positions with people that he could consider reliable whatever their own experience. There was a reaction within Iranian political circles and Mr Ahmadinejad had particular problems in getting approval from the Majlis (parliament) for some of the ministerial appointments. Bearing in mind that the theocratic power base had done much to ensure that the Majlis was dominated by conservatives, this might seem surprising. What it does show is that any internal conflict between Mr Ahmadinejad's administration and other elements of the Iranian political system is not a conventional conflict between reformers and conservatives, but more between two different versions of relatively hard-line politics.

This comes in the context of the strongly held view across Iranian society that the country has every right to promote a civil nuclear power programme, not least as a sign of modernity. It has become an indicator of national status embraced not just by Mr Ahmadinejad but by Mr Rafsanjani and many of those within the theocracy. Where there may well be a difference is in the pragmatism of the latter when it comes to international affairs. Leaders such as Mr Rafsanjani would, if in power, be handling the developing crisis in a much more subtle way – keeping the rhetoric down, avoiding diplomatic confrontations and maintaining a semblance of agreement with the International Atomic Energy Agency so as to make it difficult for Washington to adopt an aggressive stance.

The Ahmadinejad administration is certainly not doing this, not least through extreme statements directed at Israel. Moreover, these come on top of the changes in personnel described above and may suggest a degree of political naivety stemming from inexperience in foreign affairs. At the same time, it may well be that Mr Ahmadinejad and his advisors positively want a crisis with the United States, believing that this will be a powerful unifying force within Iran. This analysis is certainly supported by the careful recent statements of Mr Rafsanjani, where he has indicated support for the administration in the face of the more hard-line approach being adopted by the United States.

The view from Washington

On the face of it, the possibility of a crisis with Iran that results in a military confrontation would seem to be the last thing wanted by the US military. It is far more concerned with severe overstretch, especially in the Army, and is seeking to cut back its commitments in Iraq and Afghanistan. To contemplate military action against Iran must surely be an exercise in military stupidity.

There is one immediate counter to this view. Action to destroy Iran's nuclear programme would be very different from the involvements in Iraq and Afghanistan and would be almost entirely a matter of the use of air power and sea-borne stand-off weapons such as cruise missiles. There is little or no overstretch in these elements of the US armed forces – indeed there are almost certainly elements in the US Navy and Air Force that would welcome a role in order to focus attention on their capabilities, given the current attention being paid to the Army and Marine Corps. One of the effects of the ongoing war in Iraq is that it is these two branches of the armed forces that are getting most of the additional defence spending. Within the politics of the US military there is a constant jockeying for position, influence and resources – the Army and the Marines may be hard-pressed but it does mean that they are doing well out of current defence spending. Getting the spotlight back on the Air Force and Navy could be no bad thing from their perspective.

This does nothing to reduce the risk that a military confrontation with Iran could develop into a sustained conflict, so it does not explain the absolute insistence of the Bush administration that Iran cannot be allowed to proceed on its presumed path towards nuclear weapons. The explanation for that outlook has much more to do with longer-term issues of US strategy in the region. In part, this does still stem from the US experience in the late 1970s, when an apparently secure client regime controlled by the late Shah was overthrown in a manner that was as unexpected as it was violent. The hostage crisis, in particular, still resonates in Washington.

More generally, though, the problems in Iraq and Afghanistan have to be factored into the issue of Iran. Three years ago, the Taliban regime had been ousted in Afghanistan, al-Qaida appeared to have been dispersed and the Bush administration was set to terminate the Saddam Hussein regime in Iraq, replacing it with a client state following free market principles. Iran was still the major obstacle to US control of Gulf security, but with the onset of secure US control of Iraq and Afghanistan, to the west and east of Iran, there was little doubt that any regime in Tehran would be careful in its relations with the United States.

It is all so different now. Not only has the insurgency in Iraq persisted in a manner that has exceeded just about all military expectations,[10] but political developments are ensuring that Mr Ahmadinejad's government could have substantial influence in the future of the country. Meanwhile, Afghanistan is also far from peace, a situation made worse by the uncertainties in Pakistan. There is little sign of the situations in Iraq or Afghanistan easing, and the end result is that the United States could be faced, in two or three years' time, with a deeply troubled region in which it cannot maintain control, coupled with a vigorously independent Iran that is getting close to having the ability to produce nuclear weapons.

Iran may not choose to do so, but the development of a substantial civil nuclear power and research programme, especially if it involves a complete nuclear fuel cycle, would give it the potential to do so quite rapidly whenever it decided. The Bush administration is simply not prepared to allow this, even if Iran is within its rights under the Non-Proliferation Treaty, to develop civil nuclear power. The huge geo-strategic significance of Gulf oil reserves is such that the United States under its current leadership will not contemplate an Iran under the current or any similar regime that even has the capability to take the nuclear weapons route.

Moreover, this is not just an issue for the Republicans – recent opinion polling in the United States suggests majority support for military action against Iran in spite of the experiences in Iraq. Perhaps more indicative is the recently changed attitude of one of the leading Democrat contenders for the White House in 2008 – Hilary Clinton. She is now taking a much harder line on maintaining control of Iraq while calling for strong action against Iran.

Perhaps the one issue that is not appreciated sufficiently in Western Europe is the effect of the Shah's fall, and of the hostage crisis, more than a quarter of a century ago. In its own way, that is a much greater explanation for the origins of the current crisis than is commonly realised, and is one of the main reasons why military action, with all its dangerous consequences, may still be difficult to avoid.

11
Iraq, Three Years on – February 2006

Earlier briefings in this series sought to analyse the manner in which the United States' forces were responding to the insurgency in Iraq. In the October and November briefings last year, for example, two trends were singled out. One has been the tendency to embark on major operations against particular urban centres of the insurgency, seeking to clear these of opposition and then maintain security by a combination of US and Iraqi government forces. The assault on Fallujah in November 2004 was one of the first examples of this, but there have been many more, including Tal Afar late last year.

The other developing tactic has been to rely more heavily on helicopter gun-ships and strike aircraft to attack identified concentrations of insurgents. One of the aims here is to minimise the necessity for extensive ground patrols by US troops, but an inevitable consequence, given the frequently inadequate intelligence available on the insurgency, is an increased risk of civilian casualties.

Nevertheless, minimising US casualties is regarded as one of the key necessities for military operations, not least because of the steadily increasing impact of the deaths and serious injuries among troops on domestic opinion in the United States. By the end of February, US forces had lost almost 2,300 people killed and just under 17,000 injured in combat. Since the war started, around 10,000 troops have been medically evacuated back to the United States for treatment via the military hospital at Landstuhl in Germany. In addition, around 25,000 US personnel have been evacuated back to the United States either for non-combat injuries or through physical or mental illness.

These figures may be small compared with the losses in Korea or Vietnam, but those were when the United States had very large conscript armed forces, whereas these losses are being incurred in a smaller volunteer Army and Marine Corps, together with heavy reliance on reservists and National Guard units. The overall effect of these current trends is that the great majority of troops that have been deployed in Iraq have had personal experience of friends killed or seriously injured, and they have been facing a determined and effective urban insurgency that has proven extremely difficult to counter. Moreover, consistent attempts to train Iraqi forces to take over have been met with numerous problems of unreliability. It is this context that does much to explain the behaviour of US troops in many circumstances, with that behaviour often exacerbating the insurgency.[1]

The Significance of Samarra

One of the most damaging incidents during February was the destruction of the shrine in Samarra, an event that resulted in many hundreds of people being killed in violence across much of central Iraq.[2] The attack on the mosque was almost certainly designed to provoke conflict between Shi'a and Sunni communities, making it even less likely that the government that was in process of formation in Baghdad would successfully integrate the different confessional groups.

Whether the Samarra attack does have that impact in the longer term remains to be seen, but the city itself was important for other reasons. After the takeover of Fallujah by US forces in November 2004, Samarra became a centre of insurgency actions, and the US forces responded in the early part of 2005 by putting in large forces of their own troops together with Iraqi security units. The city was surrounded by rapidly constructed earthworks which, in combination with a limited number of checkpoints, meant that movement in and out of the city could be carefully controlled.

In this way, Samarra was seen as an example of how to curb the insurgency, yet within a few months it was apparent that the policy was not working. Because of the restrictions, about half of the population of Samarra moved away and the economy came close to collapse. Even under the tightly controlled security measures, the insurgency continued in the city with US forces taking casualties as they engaged in conflicts with insurgent groups.

As a result of the 'embedding' of an experienced journalist with a US unit, one particular incident came to light which is indicative of the problems facing the US military authorities. After one exchange of fire, two insurgents were killed, after which a sergeant ordered their bodies to be tied to the bonnets of Humvees and taken through the streets, like deer killed in a hunt. The reporter described the sullen expressions on the face of local Iraqis as they witnessed this.[3]

To the US troops involved in this operation, the insurgents were terrorists, part of a large and amorphous enemy that killed or maimed other American soldiers and was proving almost impossible to counter. Young soldiers were seeing their friends and comrades killed or horribly injured in a campaign in which they may have initially believed they were bringing democracy to Iraq, as well as facing up to an enemy which, in some indefinable way, was part of the greater enemy that had committed the 9/11 atrocities. The behaviour of tying the dead Iraqis to their vehicles may have been deeply provocative to local Iraqis, but for the soldiers concerned it was their way of retaliating against the community from which these terrorists arose, demonstrating the extent of US military power and showing the determination of the United States to maintain control.

To the Iraqis watching this in Samarra the outlook was almost diametrically opposed. What they saw was the gruesome defiling of the bodies of freedom fighters who had given their lives while resisting the occupation of their city by the foreign invaders that were being aided by collaborating Iraqis from a corrupt and unrepresentative government. The effect of this one incident is not clear, but it is part of a pattern of actions by US forces increasingly frustrated by their lack of success.

Another example is the ready recourse to massive firepower. If an American patrol comes under fire from a single sniper hidden in a building, the patrol may immediately respond with many hundreds of rounds of machine gun or cannon fire, quite possibly followed by an air strike called in to respond to the attack. From a US perspective this is a response that is fully in tune with the circumstances, a legitimate response that demonstrates both the power of the US forces in responding to terrorism and, in particular, the near-absolute requirements to minimise their own casualties. Moreover, the continual linking of the conflict in Iraq to the wider 'global war on terror' by the Bush administration, gives ordinary US troops the right to respond with such force. They are, from their perspective, not so much occupying a foreign country but protecting their own, having suffered a grievous and unprovoked attack on 11 September 2001.

From the perspective of the local Iraqi community, the end result may be the destruction of houses, factories, schools or public buildings and the likely killing of innocent people in addition to insurgents who are regarded as freedom fighters. The extent of the destruction in towns such as Tal Afar and Samarra is considerable. In Fallujah, a large proportion of all the buildings in a city of close to 300,000 people were either destroyed or badly damaged. While the US authorities played down the level of Iraqi casualties, these are now believed to have numbered close to 5,000. Of the several thousand men detained by US and Iraqi forces during the assault on Fallujah, the great majority were quickly released. This gave the lie to the idea that the only people left in the city were insurgents, with the implication that many of the 5,000 killed were civilians, not insurgents.

The Cost of the War

In Iraq itself, the estimates for civilian casualties exceed 30,000 killed and many tens of thousands seriously injured. In some parts of Iraq, conventional law and order has largely broken down – in Baghdad alone, for example, there are currently around 50 kidnappings every day. Furthermore, the insurgency continues to include the sustained use of economic targeting, especially against oil facilities. The effect of this has been to cripple Iraq's economic development. Oil production in early 2006 was still markedly lower than at the end of the Saddam Hussein regime, even though that was operating under sanctions. This has had knock-on effects across the economy with access to drinking water down by a quarter since the start of the war, and electricity supplies in Baghdad down to under four hours a day, a quarter of the level before the war.

The sustained use of economic targeting by insurgents has been achieved in spite of intensive efforts to train Iraqi security forces and the continuing presence of well over 150,000 coalition troops in the country. Estimates from the Bush administration towards the end of February spoke of 227,000 Iraqi troops and security forces available for duty, so that the combined forces available to the US and Iraqi authorities were close to 400,000.[4] While there remains tension and some violence in southern and south-eastern Iraq, this is not at the level of an all-out insurgency, and the Kurdish north-east is largely calm.

In effect, the insurgency is limited to four provinces centred on Baghdad and the towns and cities to the north and east of the capital. Within this population, the Sunni communities from which the insurgency largely draws its support number at most 6 million people, of whom no more than 2 million are adult males. While the Iraqi and US security forces are stretched across the country, at least half are deployed in this particular region in which the insurgency is concentrated. There are therefore about 200,000 troops and security personnel seeking to control an insurgency whose active paramilitaries are drawn from 2 million people, an extraordinary ratio of one soldier or security officer for every ten adult males in the entire population. Bearing in mind that perhaps half of the security personnel are US soldiers equipped with a wide range of weapons and surveillance equipment, the deep-seated and embedded nature of the insurgency begins to become apparent.

The US Defence Budget

The impact of this war, and the continuing violence in Afghanistan, is reflected not just in the human costs but also in the losses in equipment including tanks and helicopters, with this, in turn, reflected in burgeoning defence budgets. Since the start of operations in Iraq almost three years ago, the US forces have lost 20 M1 Abrams main battle tanks, 50 Bradley fighting vehicles, 20 of the new Stryker armoured fighting vehicles and 20 M113 armoured personnel carriers.[5] Almost all of these have been lost to roadside bombs, the so-called improvised explosive devices, with the recently deployed shaped-charge explosives being readily capable of attacking heavily armoured vehicles. The losses of more lightly-armoured vehicles are much higher, with some 750 Humvees, reconnaissance vehicles and transport trucks destroyed so far.

The extent of the losses, especially among tanks and armoured vehicles may seem surprising, given that the Iraq War is assumed to be a counter-insurgency operation against lightly armed paramilitaries. They are explained, in part by the fact that many of the insurgents had previous training in the armed forces of the Saddam Hussein regime, and partly by the availability of numerous munitions stored throughout central Iraq towards the end of the regime or secreted away during the chaos that immediately followed its termination.

More significantly, though, US military planners now recognise that the commitment of the insurgents and their overall morale are both much higher than had been previously understood. In the few assessments of US officers on the ground being published in some of the specialist defence journals in recent months, one aspect comes through repeatedly – the manner in which new people immediately come into the insurgency to replace those killed or detained. Given that around 25,000 suspected insurgents were killed or detained during each of the calendar years 2004 and 2005, and that many of the detentions were for months or years, with a current population of insurgent detainees of around 15,000, it is clear that this is an insurgency that is deeply embedded in a largely supportive community.

A feature of the past three years since the war started has been the increase in the basic US defence budget coupled with the supplemental requests to cover the added costs of the wars in Iraq and Afghanistan. Following a decrease in the defence budget in the 1990s after the collapse of the Soviet Union, the budgets are now approaching the exceptionally high levels of the most intense period of the Cold War in the mid-1980s.

The first big increase came in 2003, with a total spending of $455 billion, compared with $362 billion the previous year. Two years later, the Fiscal Year 2005 budget reached $520 billion, with a basic budget of $420 billion and supplementals for war costs of another $100 billion. The supplementals for the current FY 2006 period (October 2005 to September 2006) amount to $115 billion on a basic budget of just over $440 billion. With a total defence expenditure for the year of $556.8 billion we are now at levels that compare with Cold War peaks.

There is, though, one important difference. At the height of the Cold War, the United States maintained much larger forces, including a 500-ship Navy, very large heavily-armoured ground forces in Western Europe and strategic and tactical nuclear forces of over 20,000 weapons. These were directed at facing down the Soviet Union, then seen as a massively resourced superpower that had to be met on a more or less equal footing. Whatever the realities of actual Soviet power, US defence policy and budgets reflected a response to a formidable enemy with millions of troops at its disposal.

Now, the United States faces a few tens of thousands of insurgents in Iraq and Afghanistan, with the prospect of a conflict with a state, Iran, which does not even remotely begin to compare in military power even with US forces in the region. Even under these circumstances, the United States is facing severe overstretch in its Army and Marine Corps while it faces substantial increases in its defence budget in order to try and control protracted insurgencies.

For now, though, there are few indications of any substantial rethinking of military strategies. Indeed, the publication of the Quadrennial Defence Review in February showed a commitment of more of the same. Donald Rumsfeld's characterisation of the new era as a 'Long War' replacing the 'Cold War' is indicative of the persistence of the current security paradigm.[6] As we move towards the fourth year of the Iraq War, there is little or no sign of change.

12
Iran, Sliding to War? – March 2006

Afghanistan

During March there were increasing security problems in Afghanistan with the possibility of a Taliban 'spring offensive' growing (see Chapter 10). Activities by Taliban and other militias increased, with a number of attacks on the International Security Assistance Force (ISAF) and US forces, but the much greater problem was the series of near-daily attacks on Afghan security forces and government officials. These included eleven major incidents during the course of the month, most commonly aimed at police, security and intelligence personnel, but a particular feature was the pattern of assassination attempts on senior figures.

On 12 March, two suicide bombers attacked the vehicle carrying Sibghatullah Mujadidi, the Leader of the Upper House of Parliament, killing two civilians and injuring Mr Mujadidi. The attack may have had a particular significance as he was head of a government commission that was attempting to negotiate with Taliban elements with a view to seeking reconciliation. On 18 March, assassination attempts were made on the governor of Ghazni province and the previous governor. The current governor survived but his predecessor, Qari Baba, was killed along with four other people. Four days later the governor of the province of Faryab survived an attack.[1]

March also saw a number of attacks on aid organisations and private security personnel, as well as a deterioration in the security situation along the Afghanistan/Pakistan border as tensions between the two countries increased.[2] Afghan officials claimed that Pakistani security forces were not doing enough to provide security in the frontier districts, but the Pakistani government responded by pointing to 82,000 Army troops deployed along the border.

Independent analyses point to the failure of the Pakistani Army to control the region, especially the districts of North and South Waziristan. Over the past three years there have been attempts by the authorities to deal with local elders, encouraging them to give up radical elements. By and large, these have failed, and there have been two unfortunate consequences from Pakistan's point of view. One is that there has been an increased anti-government mood, made worse by the effects of US unmanned aerial drones targeting presumed Taliban groups but often killing civilians. President Musharraf is regarded as being far too close to the United States, and the result of US actions such as these within the country is to heighten the mood of antagonism.[3]

The second consequence has been that the independent power base of the elders in the frontier districts has been weakened by what is seen as the more direct interference by government. The previous pattern was for them to exercise considerable power and influence but they are now being replaced by a new generation of younger men, often closely allied to militias that connect with Taliban groups. Up until about three years ago, the Pakistani government tacitly allowed elders in the frontier region effective control, but that has now partially ended, eroding the power of the elders in favour of this new generation.

The end result of this is that the frontier region is simply not under the control of the Pakistani Army, whatever may be claimed by Islamabad. A full-scale spring offensive in Afghanistan by

Taliban and other militias has not yet developed, but there has certainly been a marked deterioration in security across substantial parts of the country, together with a weakening of the authority of Musharraf's regime in Pakistan.

Iraq

At the time of the elections four months ago, there was a concerted effort by the Bush administration to put forward the view that Iraq was moving towards a more peaceful era. This has simply been eroded by the substantial rise in sectarian violence in addition to the existing insurgency and rampant criminality. During the course of March there was much controversy over whether the security situation in Iraq had degenerated into a civil war. Whatever definition one uses of a civil war, such terminology is singularly unhelpful in that it does not matter hugely in analysing the recent developments.[4]

What is clear is that there has been a general deterioration in the levels of security in much of the country. A US government assessment at the end of March was that the situation in six of Iraq's 18 provinces was serious and, in one case, was critical. As the provinces included the largest population centre, Baghdad, and another major centre, Basra, the assessment was that about half of the entire population was living in these insecure areas. This compared with four provinces said to be heavily affected by the insurgency just a year ago. Moreover, the new assessment also downgraded the security situation in Basra, a city that had previously been relatively calm.

Four issues stand out. One is that March did see a decrease in US combat deaths, although the level of combat injuries was as high as ever.[5] Given that the United States is conducting fewer ground patrols and is relying more on air power, it is not surprising that combat deaths have decreased. This trend may be used in Washington as a sign of improvement, but two further factors discount this. One is that attacks on Iraqi security forces have been particularly severe, and another is that the number of kidnappings and sectarian murders has increased substantially in recent months, including around 50 inter-communal killings every day.

The fourth issue has been the rise to greater prominence of Shi'a militia, especially the Mahdi Army that has allegiance to Moqtada al-Sadr. This group and other militias have some links with Iran, especially the Iranian Revolutionary Guard, and US military and political sources have made much of Iran's involvement in the insurgency. In fact, there is little evidence of any substantive involvement, but that does not disguise the fact that Iranian interests could greatly aid insurgent actions against the United States if they chose to do so.

Whatever happens in the coming months in Iraq, there are no indications whatsoever of a wholesale United States withdrawal from the country. There may well be a draw down of a few thousand troops in the run-up to the November Congressional elections, but this relates to US domestic politics. What is more revealing is a series of reports that the United States is investing heavily in building programmes that allow for long-term basing of US troops at a number of key sites in Iraq.[6] In this respect there has been no change in policy. What is still sought is a stable pro-American client government in power in Baghdad, with the United States maintaining perhaps 20,000 troops in the country and acting as a final guarantor of Iraqi government stability. In the current circumstances such an aim is implausible in the extreme, but there are no indications of any alternative policies coming out of Washington even if the war is now into its fourth year.[7]

Iran

In Chapter 10 it was suggested that the potential for conflict over Iran's nuclear ambitions would become progressively more prominent during the course of 2006. Two months later, this has proved to be the case, and it is worth standing back to get a detached view of the recent developments.[8] A starting point remains the Oxford Research Group report, *Iran: Consequences of a War*, which concluded that any US military action against Iranian nuclear facilities would be likely to lead to a complex set of Iranian responses. These could lead to major difficulties for the United States and its coalition partners in the region, coupled with the risk of a very considerable impact on world oil prices. Although many analysts and some politicians share this view, it has had little or no impact in Washington where there are a number of indications that serious planning for military action is now under way.

Given the risks that would result from American action against Iranian nuclear facilities, it is relevant to ask why Iran causes such concern in Washington. Part of the explanation does go back to the fall of the Shah. Not only was this a severe shock to the United States since the Shah's Iran had been its key client state in the region and a perceived bulwark against the Soviet Union during the Cold War era, but the manner of the revolution was an added shock. It happened with a rapidity that caught almost every part of the American government by surprise, and was made much worse by the holding of US diplomats hostage in Tehran for more than a year.

While this memory is deep-seated, especially in the State Department, it is only a partial explanation. Three other factors have to be taken into account. One is the central importance of the security of Israel to successive American administrations. Jewish support for Israel within the United States may have weakened in recent years especially as many liberal Jews became increasingly critical of the policies of the Sharon government, but this has been counterbalanced by the increased political power of the Christian Zionists and the pro-Israel neo-conservatives.

The Christian Zionists may not exhibit the political sophistication of the traditional Israel lobby but they have become an important adjunct to it, representing a sector of the electorate numbering in the tens of millions that tends to vote Republican in Congressional and Presidential elections. Israel regards Iran as its only major threat in the entire region, and has done so more or less continually since the fall of the Shah 27 years ago. It follows that US domestic support for Israel shares this view, and prominent pro-Israeli politicians in the United States are particularly strong in their rhetoric against Iran.

Iran has also become a greater problem for the United States because of the failures in Iraq. The original intention in terminating the Saddam Hussein regime was not just to get a stable client state operating pro-American free-market principles, but to do so right next to Iran and to be able to maintain permanent bases there. 'The road to Tehran goes through Baghdad' was a common saying in Washington in 2002, and the confident expectation was that US prowess in Iraq would have a profound impact in Tehran. If the United States was willing and able to terminate regimes to the east and west of Iran, and to use the Fifth Fleet to control the Persian Gulf and the Arabian Sea, then any regime in Tehran would be exceedingly cautious about developing foreign and security policies that were in any way opposed to US interests.

With the failure to achieve its objectives in Iraq, the United States has not only lost this opportunity to influence Iran, but has actually handed Tehran a substantial political gift. Iran is now free to develop close links with Iraq's Shi'a majority and can even set up a series of relationships with some of the insurgent groups.[9] It is now less a case of the United States being able to put indirect pressure on Iran, more the other way round. This is, to put it bluntly, unacceptable to Washington.

Finally, the US relationship with Iran remains deeply connected to oil security across the region. With the United States and China increasingly reliant on Gulf oil, and with the rest of the industrialised world similarly dependent, the Persian Gulf is just too important for Washington to allow an independent 'rogue state' to enhance its power base. As a result, the view from within the Bush administration is that there are no circumstances under which Iran can be allowed to become a nuclear weapons power. Not only is this unacceptable, but Iran cannot even be allowed to have the theoretical capability to develop nuclear weapons. It follows that the development of a full nuclear fuel cycle, even if the ostensible motive is to support a civil nuclear power programme, cannot be allowed.

The Tehran Perspective

From within Iran, the thirst for technological modernity is such that just such a civil nuclear power programme is seen as an absolute right for a country of 75 million people and a 3,000-year history that intends to embrace the twenty-first century. Given the regime's theocratic nature this may seem a surprise, but that view fails to understand the nature of the theocracy. In Iranian religious thinking, what may appear to some other cultures to be a near-medieval return to religious rigidity is seen as a purification process that is in no way in contradiction to the development of advanced technologies. Indeed, such progress will serve to enhance the potential for the further development of society – Islamist modernity is not seen as a contradiction in terms.

With this at the root of the political outlook there is the added perception of an evil opposing superpower that is absolutely determined to prevent Iran achieving its potential. This superpower has already characterised Iran as part of an 'axis of evil' and a 'rogue state' and is openly financing opposition groups that are seeking regime change. In such circumstances, military strength, including at least the theoretical capability to take the nuclear weapons route, is seen as a matter of routine political sense. That this is the case with a regime that is currently led by a man given to extreme statements regarding Israel means that there is a clear risk of a US/Iran confrontation.

Allies of the United States may be very keen to avoid such a confrontation, and considerable efforts may be made to use diplomatic pressure and even economic sanctions against Iran rather than a military confrontation.[10] It is not clear, however, if the Iranians will respond to the former, given the rhetoric coming out of Washington, and sanctions have little prospect of being effective given the long-term oil and gas deals that Iran has recently concluded with China and India.

One positive indication is that some European governments do seem to appreciate the considerable dangers that would arise following any American military action against Iranian nuclear facilities. Iran's capacity for retaliation in Iraq, in western Gulf states and against oil exports from the Gulf is clearly recognised in a number of European capitals where it is believed that the consequences could be far greater than those now being experienced in Iraq. Whatever may be said in public, there are likely to be intensive private efforts by some European governments to restrain the Bush administration from any precipitate action, no matter how deep-seated are the administration's concerns over Iran.

At root, though, the tensions remain and will not easily be diminished. It is in these circumstances that it is necessary to be prepared for the unexpected. Given the mutual antagonism between Tehran and Washington, quite small incidents are easily capable of turning problems into crises. That may be the main danger in the coming months as wiser political counsels attempt to avert a full-scale confrontation.

13
From Cold War to Long War – April 2006

In recent months, the term 'Long War' has been used more and more frequently by senior Pentagon officials to characterise the global 'war on terror' and to give it a status similar to that of the Cold War. The use of such a phrase implies a long and potentially difficult conflict that requires persistence and patriotism. One particular value is that the idea that the United States is fighting a long war for its very security means that loyalty is taken as a norm. For much of the Cold War it was not acceptable to see the Soviet Union as anything other than an 'evil empire'. Similarly the 'axis of evil' and the terrorist threat from al-Qaida has to be seen as a circumstance beyond discussion – there are no alternatives to fighting this war and to think otherwise is at best misguided and at worst malign.

During the course of April there were significant developments in all three major aspects of this Long War – al-Qaida, Iraq and Afghanistan – as well as the consolidation of the military approaches to be applied in the coming years. In many respects the deterioration in the levels of security in Iraq and Afghanistan might be expected to lead to a re-thinking of the overall approach, but as the Iraq War entered its fourth year and the overall 'war on terror' headed towards its sixth year, there was little sign of that.

Al-Qaida

The movement usually characterised by the term 'al-Qaida' is diffuse and multifaceted. Leaders and strategists such as bin Laden and al-Zawahiri communicate through video and audio tapes and have a following across much of the world, but it is by no means clear that they have a major influence on the policies and tactics of individual groups. This is almost certainly the case in Egypt, where there was yet another attack, this time at the small tourist resort of Dahab on the Red Sea Coast of Sinai on 24 April. Three bombs were detonated killing 23 people and injuring 62, most of them Egyptians.[1]

The Dahab attack was the fifth in the immediate region in the past 18 months, four of them in less than a year and three of them against targets in Sinai. The first, in October 2005, was the bombing of the Taba Hilton and a campsite close to the Israeli border and a resort much frequented by Israeli tourists. This was followed in July 2005 by multiple bombings of two hotels and a market place in Sharm al-Sheikh at the southern tip of the Sinai peninsula, a town that has been the location of major meetings on the Israel/Palestine issue.

The following month it was the Jordanian port of Aqaba that was the location for a failed attempt to damage US warships with Katyusha rockets, and in November a series of bombings of three western hotels in Amman killed 57 people. Most recently came the Dahab bombing, with all the incidents showing a concern with western, Israeli or tourist-orientated targets.

More generally, they represented persistent attacks in two highly pro-western states that are considered by militants to be run by undemocratic elites, it being one of the long-term aims of the broad al-Qaida movement to replace such power structures with what would be considered legitimate Islamist rule. One of the main areas of significance for the attacks was that both Egypt and Jordan had very tight security structures yet these were unable to prevent the attacks even in the face of widespread arrests and detention without trial of radical elements.

The Abqaiq Attack

Four weeks before the Dahab attack, another incident, this time in Saudi Arabia, had a significance that was not widely recognised at the time – on 24 February 2006 an attempt was made to damage an oil facility at Abqaiq close to the Persian Gulf coast of Saudi Arabia. The attack failed, or at least official news reports indicated failure, but the significance lies more in the nature of the target. Saudi Arabia has the world's largest oil reserves and is also the largest exporter. Most of the fields are located close to the Persian Gulf coast and two-thirds of Saudi Arabia's total crude oil production goes through a single plant at Abqaiq. Described as the jewel in the crown of the Saudi oil industry, Abqaiq processes 'sour' crude into 'sweet' crude mainly by removing hydrogen sulphide in a series of huge hydrogen-desulphurisation towers.

The plant was attacked by a suicide squad driving two car bombs, supported by a 4x4 attack vehicle. Guards were killed by gunfire and the explosions, but the company running the plant, Aramco, claimed that neither of the car bombs detonated within the main plant, even though early press reports spoke of a fire within the plant. The lack of damage has been disputed by local sources that claim that one car got into the main plant, missing the most important facilities but causing substantial damage. In any case, the key point is that the Abqaiq attack was the first occasion in which a heavily guarded oil plant was attacked in Saudi Arabia. It may well indicate a change of tactics by regional paramilitary groups that recognise the remarkable effects of the continuing disruption of the oil industry across the border in Iraq.

Iraq

Within Iraq itself the modest political progress towards establishing a functioning administration was overshadowed by continuing violence. After the low US casualties in March, the losses were more than doubled in April to 76 killed, with over 400 injured in the same period. The Iraqi casualties were massively higher, with an Iraqi government report of 1,091 people killed in Baghdad alone. While Baghdad has been the central focus of car bombings, kidnappings and death squads, there has been violence in many other towns and cities, and it is probable that the numbers killed in the insurgency and in sectarian conflict across the country are at least double those of the Baghdad area.[2]

If this level of violence is maintained, then Iraq will be experiencing up to 25,000 deaths a year, with many tens of thousands of people injured as well. The US and UK governments have been deeply reluctant to conduct what are termed 'body counts' but in recent months have had to admit to over 30,000 civilians killed. These figures are assumed to have come from the Iraq Body Count group that uses an exacting media research methodology requiring specific media casualty reports from more than one source.

This has one major advantage in that it is very difficult for occupying powers to denigrate the figures, and Iraq Body Count was particularly important in the first 12–18 months of the war when the reluctance on the part of military and political leaders to discuss the issue was at its height. At the same time, the Iraq Body Count figures are best seen as baseline figures and the group itself makes the point that the true figures may be very much higher. Even so, the Iraq Body Count assessment is now heading towards 40,000 killed and if the recent indicative figures for Baghdad are taken into account, this will grow rapidly in the coming months.

There have been repeated claims from the Bush administration that the political progress in Iraq, slow as it has been, does actually presage an increase in stability.[3] This is a particularly important line to take as it suggests that troop withdrawals will be possible before the mid-sessional elections to Congress in November. Behind this suggestion is the implied possibility that the United States could withdraw more or less completely from Iraq in the relatively near future, perhaps less than five years. Given the increasing unpopularity of the war within the United States, the idea of disengagement rather than just partial troop withdrawals seems attractive.

The problem with this line of thinking is that it simply does not match with what is happening on the ground in Iraq.[4] Shortly after the termination of the Saddam Hussein regime just over three years ago, the *New York Times* ran a piece about plans to construct four permanent 'super-bases'. One would be adjacent to Baghdad, two would be close to the northern and southern oil fields and one would be in the west towards Syria and close to anticipated areas of oil exploration in the western desert. The report was largely discounted and there have been strenuous denials from Washington of any plans to stay long term – indeed 'permanent' is now a term that is banned from the discourse.

The reality is very different, with abundant evidence that the *New York Times* piece was broadly correct. The four bases are all being built up from infrastructure originating in four of the Saddam Hussein regime's large airfields, with all of them away from major urban areas, making them easier to defend from insurgents. The largest in terms of current troop dispositions is Balad, to the north of Baghdad, and the other three are al-Asad in the west, Tallil in the south and al-Qayyarah in the north. All are being comprehensively re-equipped for air operations and there is a progressive replacement of temporary trailer accommodation with permanent buildings.

As the bases are developed, so US forces are withdrawing from smaller locations and, in doing so, are able to reconfigure in two different ways to add to their security. One is that bases such as Balad have very large taxi-ways and hard-standings, combined with re-engineered and strengthened runways, so that they can take the largest transport aircraft. This means that re-provision is less dependent on vulnerable road transport. The second aspect is that the move towards relying on helicopter gun-ships and fixed-wing strike aircraft for supporting counter-insurgency operations is made much easier. Balad alone has space for 120 helicopters, allowing the US forces to position helicopters across much of the most violent parts of central Iraq within 30 minutes.[5]

The inevitable result of the move towards heavy reliance on air power is an increase in civilian casualties, with the further inevitable result of an increase in anti-American feeling, but this is viewed as a necessary consequence of the essential need to cut down on US casualties. It is in this context that the continuing high levels of US troop deaths and injuries are so significant. If the unusually low level of deaths among American troops in March had been the start of a trend, then the military and political leaders could cite this as proof of the viability of the changed policy, whatever the other effects. The early indications are that they cannot even do this.

More generally, the four bases do show pretty conclusively that the United States intends to stay in Iraq for many years to come. This is further supported by the current building of the world's largest embassy in Baghdad. Constructed, like the bases, primarily by foreign contractors (in this case Kuwait), the embassy will be a massive self-contained and heavily protected compound immediately adjacent to the Iraqi seat of government and close to most ministries. As with the bases, the clear implication is that if the insurgency is finally contained and if a civil war is avoided, then the United States will maintain a dominant relationship with future Iraqi administrations dependent, in the final analysis, on the presence of up to 40,000 US troops at permanent bases. All this, though, presupposes an end to the war, and there is no sign of that at present.

Afghanistan

As anticipated in earlier briefings in this series, there is currently an increase in paramilitary activities in Afghanistan as Taliban and other insurgent groups increase the number of attacks. These are directed against Afghan police and security forces, government officials and offices, foreign contractors and some aid personnel, and troops from the International Security Assistance Force and the US counter-insurgency forces.[6] It now looks probable that a sustained offensive is evolving, aided by the manner in which paramilitary groups now control significant parts of the Pakistani districts close to the border such as North and South Waziristan. This control allows the militias a high degree of freedom to move each way across the border, but the whole paramilitary offensive is also being aided by the availability of increasing amounts of finance stemming from the opium/heroin trade in Afghanistan.

If one of the aims of support for a civil Afghan government has been to bring opium poppy cultivation under control, then this has been a conspicuous failure, with production now at levels typical of some of the peak periods of the 1990s. Early indications are that the current poppy harvest will be based on one of the largest ever acreages of cultivation, but the more indicative trend has been towards the refining of raw opium into heroin and morphine within Afghanistan itself. This is a recent development but has the important result that the entire trade becomes far more lucrative, since refined products are hugely more profitable. This in turn stems from the profits made by smuggling precursor chemicals into Afghanistan to be used in the refining process, together with the mark-ups that arise from the actual refining process itself.

Many of the stages in heroin production, from cultivation through to access to precursor chemicals and on to refining, are under the direct or indirect control of warlords, criminal groups and paramilitaries. For the Taliban and similar groups, the entire process enables them to access new sources of income to support the insurgency, whether that be in the form of weapons, munitions, food, transport and other supplies, bribes to drugs trade participants and to government officials or simply wages for insurgents. What it adds up to is an escalating problem for the Afghan government and foreign forces from the United States, Britain and elsewhere. The end result is that Afghanistan is simply not experiencing the transition to peace and security that was originally expected.

The Long War

Although the problems in Iraq and Afghanistan are substantial, and the al-Qaida movement and its associates continue their activities, all the indications are that US defence strategy will concentrate on the enhancement of existing capabilities rather than conducting any substantive re-assessment of policies. The Fiscal Year 2007 Defense Budget is a clear indicator of this, as is the new Quadrennial Defense Review (QDR). In the immediate future of the FY 2007 Budget and the longer-term time-span of the QDR, the concentration will be on military operations as the Long War evolves.[7] The emphasis will be on force projection, including the possible use of pre-emptive action against states considered a threat. There will also be a further upgrading of Special Forces, with a particular feature being the development and deployment of Special Force units attached to US Embassies in a range of countries. These units will have the capability to take action within those countries, whatever the attitudes of the governments concerned. There will also be the incorporation of unmanned combat aerial vehicles (UCAVs or armed drones) more fully into the armed forces.

In terms both of the wider use of Special Forces and the use of UCAVs, this amounts to the 'mainstreaming' of such capabilities into the US armed forces from agencies such as the CIA. It is perhaps the clearest marker of the manner in which the United States military intends to fight this Long War, in spite of all of the problems that are currently being experienced. Earlier briefings in this series have pointed to the need for a fundamental re-assessment of the conduct and likely outcome of the 'war on terror'. Instead the indications are of a hardening of policies and less concern with alternatives as the Long War begins to evolve.

14
Endless War?

Prior to the attacks in New York and Washington on 11 September 2001 the newly elected Bush administration exhibited a marked degree of confidence in terms of its foreign and security policy. The twenty-first century had the potential to be the 'New American Century', neo-conservatism was more dominant in Washington than realism and there was seen to be a clear advantage in adopting a unilateralist stance on some of the major security and foreign policy issues.[1] The 9/11 attacks therefore came as a particularly wounding shock to a political culture that was very sure of its position, and the responses were immediate and comprehensive.

Five years after the 9/11 attacks it is appropriate to analyse the nature of the responses and to compare their anticipated outcomes with actual circumstances. It is also appropriate to analyse the aims of the principal opponents of the United States and its coalition partners, especially the al-Qaida movement. In doing so it is essential to recognise the differing timescales in which the opposing groups are operating.

US Aims in the War on Terror

In responding to the 9/11 attacks, the Bush administration went well beyond the pursuit and destruction of those directly responsible to embrace other concerns such as the status and potential threats from Iraq, Iran, North Korea and other countries. As encapsulated in the 2002 State of the Union address and the West Point speech shortly afterwards, the response included the identification of an 'axis of evil' involving a series of rogue states that supported terrorism and were also engaged in the development of weapons of mass destruction, together with a forceful policy of being willing to pre-empt future threats from those states or other sources. The term 'global war on terror' was employed from a very early stage and there was no pretence that it would be only a matter of months before all threats to the United States were removed. At the same time, it is possible to assess the expectations in Washington at the time of the State of the Union address in January 2002, to place these in the context of the major opponents, and then analyse the evolving situation some five years after the 9/11 attacks.

From the standpoint of the United States there were three requirements. One was to terminate the Taliban regime in Afghanistan as the host to the al-Qaida movement, and a second was to cripple the movement and its affiliates to the extent that they would no longer present a particular threat to the continental United States and its interests overseas. Finally, it was necessary either to effect regime change in the principal rogue states of Iraq and Iran or at least so constrain their activities as to diminish any threat they might be thought to pose.

It proved possible to terminate the Taliban regime in Afghanistan with relative ease, the process being completed by the end of 2002. As discussed in Chapter 1, regime termination was achieved not through the large-scale deployment of ground forces but through three linked policies. One was the use of the overwhelming air power advantage available to US forces, extending from precision-guided munitions through to area attacks using high-flying B-1 and B-52 strategic bombers. Strike aircraft were deployed from bases in the region and from aircraft carriers in the Arabian Sea, and strategic bombers flew from bases in the United States, Britain and Diego Garcia.

The extent to which precision-guided munitions were used was not fully appreciated at the time, but the drain on supplies of these munitions was such that stocks held in reserve in Kuwait and elsewhere had to be used in Afghanistan. As a result, throughout much of 2002, munitions companies in the United States had to work at a high rate to replenish supplies. It is worth noting that this presented a technical limitation on the possibility of early military action against Iraq. During the middle and latter part of 2002, there was extensive coverage of diplomatic moves to develop a coalition for action against Iraq, much of it focused on discussions at the United Nations. Many commentators saw this as an essential political process to prepare the way for the termination of the Saddam Hussein regime, implying that such termination could not otherwise go ahead. Whether or not this is correct, it is also the case that the United States was not militarily ready to go to war with Iraq until the end of 2002, because of the shortage of specialised air-delivered munitions.

In terms of the air war in Afghanistan, this was aided by the second aspect, the extensive use of Special Forces, not least for target identification for aircraft. The US Special Forces also played an important role in what was the most significant aspect of US strategy in Afghanistan in late 2001 – the re-arming and general logistical support for the Northern Alliance forces. Although the Taliban movement had first emerged in Afghanistan in 1994 and had succeeded in capturing Kabul in September 1996, it never gained complete control of the country. Even by 2001 it was still engaged in a bitter civil war with a coalition of warlords and others known as the Northern Alliance. There were ethnic elements to this since the Taliban movement was primarily drawn from Pashtuns in central and eastern Afghanistan and western Pakistan, but Taliban control stretched beyond the Pashtun-dominated areas of Afghanistan, with the Northern Alliance restricted to the northern part of the country.

During the course of October and November 2002, the United States worked to ensure the substantial strengthening of the Northern Alliance, with much of the re-arming and re-equipping coming from Russian and Central Asian sources, although financed primarily by the United States. The end result was that the combination of a revitalised Northern Alliance, US air power and the deployment of Special Forces rapidly tipped the balance in the pre-existing Afghan Civil War against the Taliban regime, resulting in the fall of that regime.

Even so, while the Taliban most certainly did allow the al-Qaida movement considerable access to facilities in Afghanistan, it was a two-way process. Afghanistan gave the diffuse al-Qaida movement a base for operations and training, but it also ensured that paramilitary supporters of the Taliban from elsewhere in the world could be trained in Afghanistan and would join with Taliban elements engaged in the civil war against the Northern Alliance. In the wake of the fall of the Taliban there was an assumption among many commentators that the loss of its Afghanistan bases would hugely cripple the al-Qaida movement in that it would lose the many training camps devoted to producing new generations of young jihadists for the wider campaign.

In practice, the al-Qaida facilities in Afghanistan should more correctly be seen in the context of the Afghan civil war rather than solely in terms of al-Qaida's longer-term aims. It was certainly the case that a successful outcome of the civil war would be valuable to al-Qaida – the very involvement of foreign jihadists in the civil war, with the combat experience they would acquire, would be to the advantage of the wider movement. But Afghanistan was simply not as essential to the movement as may have been supposed, especially given its strength in western Pakistan and the many connections across North Africa, the Middle East and Central Asia.

Little of this was recognised in Washington at the time. Instead it was believed by early 2002 that the Taliban no longer presented any regional threat to US interests and the al-Qaida movement had been seriously crippled. The expectation was that Afghanistan would make an effective transition to a stable pro-western state, a market economy would be embraced and reconstruction would be effective and aided by a number of western governments. There would also be three further benefits from the termination of the Taliban. One would be the control of rural Afghanistan as being the world's primary site of opium poppy cultivation for the production of heroin and morphine. A second would be the establishment of a small but powerful US military presence, most probably centred on two large bases. One would be at Bagram north of Kabul and the other would be close to Kandahar in the south. A future Afghanistan government would have the assurance of a continuing US military presence providing a degree of security, and the United States would have a powerful if indirect source of political influence in a strategically important state with borders stretching from Iran in the west to China in the east.

Finally, and perhaps most valuable of all, the United States had been able to establish a series of temporary bases and basing facilities in a number of Eastern European and Central Asian countries during the operations in Afghanistan in late 2001. These included facilities in Romania and Bulgaria and bases in countries such as Uzbekistan. The facilities in the Black Sea states could be of potential long-term value for two reasons – they would consolidate relations with those states, drawing them closer into the NATO fold and away from Russia, and they would provide excellent basing capabilities, especially for air movements through to the Middle East and South West Asia, reducing the US reliance on Turkey.

Developing long-term relations with Central Asian states such as Uzbekistan and Kyrgyzstan would be even more advantageous in enhancing the US presence in oil-rich Central

Asia and countering Russian and Chinese influence in the region. Although the Russian economy had come close to collapse in the early 1990s, and the Russian defence forces had not even been sufficient to contain the Chechen rebellion, there remained a concern in Washington that Russia could, at some stage, re-emerge as a significant power, given its formidable oil and natural gas reserves.

Similarly, the rapid pace of economic growth in China meant that the most substantial future challenge to US world power might come from China. Given the increasing oil import dependence of the Chinese, a greater influence for the United States in Central Asia, especially the oil-rich Caspian Basin region, could well be of value in the future balance of power with China and Russia.

In short, by early 2002, the operation in Afghanistan and the presumed weakening of al-Qaida, together with the accompanying involvements in Eastern Europe and Central Asia were seen as major advantages for the United States. In one sense, the atrocities of 9/11 had resulted in substantial military progress in longer-term issues of US security.

While the problem of North Korea was likely to remain, given its probable transition to a limited nuclear weapons status, the global war on terror could also be greatly advantageous to the United States in relation to challenges from the Saddam Hussein regime in Iraq, and the Islamist administration in Iran. The moves towards regime termination in Baghdad substantially pre-dated the 9/11 attacks and even the election of George W. Bush in November 2000.[2] Many of the significant members of the newly-formed Bush administration in January 2001 had been active in calling for a firm approach towards Iraq for several years previously, and their views entered the political mainstream with the new administration.

Moreover, the long-standing concern with Iran was also boosted by the Bush election victory. If regime change in Tehran was less prominently articulated, it was certainly the case that the enforced fall of the Saddam Hussein regime in Iraq would send a powerful message to Tehran, ensuring a quiescent regime in the face of substantial US power in the region. A phrase common in Washington at the time was that 'the road to Tehran runs through Baghdad'.

With the apparent success in Afghanistan, the likely outcome of the war on terror, as it appeared in early 2002, would therefore have a number of components:

- Afghanistan would be transformed into a viable pro-western state, with diminishing opium production and a small but long-term US military presence ensuring security and enduring US influence.
- The al-Qaida movement would be seriously damaged and the threat that it posed would be greatly reduced to the point of being manageable, even if there might be occasional further incidents away from the continental United States.
- Regime change in Iraq would be effected, with that country also transformed into a pro-western state with a vigorous market economy providing many opportunities, not least for trans-national oil corporations (TNOCs).
- In the face of major US influence and a military presence in neighbouring Iraq, Iran would be unlikely to cause problems in the region and would, effectively, be contained.

In more general terms, the impact on the Middle East would also be favourable to the United States' closest ally, Israel. Some within the Bush administration even spoke of a Greater Middle East Initiative that would bring about regime change in countries such as Syria, leading ultimately to a transition across the region resulting in reliable pro-western free market liberal democracies.

Thus the Bush administration would have been seen to have responded to the 9/11 atrocities with great vigour and certitude, bringing about a positive improvement in international security, as viewed from Washington. In one sense, the 9/11 attacks would have served the purpose of a wake-up call for the United States to reinforce its international influence for its own benefit and for that of global security as a whole – the New American Century would have been made secure.

Al-Qaida Aims and Strategies

It is inappropriate to describe the al-Qaida movement as a discrete organisation with an hierarchical structure. Terms such as franchise, consortium and network-of-networks are all more useful, and 'movement' gives the best indication of its nature. There has been a conspicuous tendency, especially in the United States, to see al-Qaida and the Taliban groups primarily in terms of their leaders. This was most noticeable in late 2001 when Osama bin Laden and the Taliban leader Mullah Omar were widely represented by the Bush administration as Public Enemies Numbers 1 and 2. Al-Qaida was seen, in particular, as a transnational yet tightly controlled and extremist organisation devoted solely to a radical religious revival largely devoid of distinct political aims.

In practice this was at best an incomplete picture, with the al-Qaida movement having quite distinct short-term aims coupled with an overarching long-term intention. The main short-term aims, as of early 2002, were:

- Eviction of foreign military forces from the Islamic world, the main emphasis being on western Gulf states, especially Saudi Arabia.
- The termination of the House of Saud in Saudi Arabia as the corrupt, illegitimate and excessively pro-western

Keeper of the Two Holy Places, and its replacement with a genuinely Islamic regime.

- The termination of elitist, corrupt and pro-western regimes across the region, with some emphasis on Egypt, Gulf emirates and Pakistan, and their replacement with genuinely Islamic regimes.
- The establishment of a Palestinian state in place of Israel.
- Support for local movements such as the Southern Thailand separatists, radical movements in Indonesia and insurgents in Indian-controlled Kashmir.

By early 2002, the al-Qaida movement could already claim some success in that most of the substantial US military forces that had been present in Saudi Arabia since the Iraqi invasion of Kuwait in 1990 were being withdrawn, with the probability of complete withdrawal within a couple of years. Moreover, given that the movement was envisaging a 10–20 year process for the achievement of even these short-term aims, temporary setbacks should not be viewed as substantive.

It is worth noting that the al-Qaida movement only embraced the Palestinian cause in the early 2000s, having not regarded it as a core aim previously. It now did so in part because of the particularly hard-line policies of the Sharon government, but its support was not greatly welcomed by most Palestinians.

Beyond this range of short-term aims, the al-Qaida movement also had the more general aim of working towards the re-establishment of an Islamic Caliphate, not necessarily modelled on the historic Caliphates such as the Abbasids a thousand years earlier but certainly embracing a politico/religious entity that would be formed initially across much of the Middle East. Such a long-term aim would be seen as a process that would stretch over 50–100 years.

Within this overall outlook, the view from within the movement was of a 'near' enemy and a 'far' enemy. The former comprised those thoroughly illegitimate and elitist regimes and their supporters in the Middle East heartland of the Islamic world. The far enemy was principally the United States, together with its closer allies such as Britain and Spain.

In such a context it is possible to argue that the movement's encouragement of those responsible for the 9/11 attacks may have had more than one motive. The most widely recognised motive would be to enhance the status of the movement by showing its capability to strike at the very heart of the far enemy, using crude but effective examples of asymmetric warfare. By contrasting the vulnerability of the world's sole superpower with the ability of the movement to strike not just in Saudi Arabia, Kenya or Tanzania, but in New York and Washington, there would be a propaganda victory that would greatly enhance the reputation of the movement among its supporters.

Second to this motive, though, may have been the intention to provoke the United States and western coalition partners into a full-scale intervention in Afghanistan, bringing in substantial numbers of ground forces to terminate the Taliban regime and subsequently occupy the country while putting in power a client regime. Given the experience against the Soviet occupation of the 1980s, this would be a case of bringing the far enemy into a zone of conflict that would enable a Taliban/al-Qaida coalition to develop a resistance movement against this new foreign occupation. This could, in due course, have had as devastating a long-term impact on the United States and its coalition partners as the expulsion of the Soviet Union had had at the end of the 1980s. The work to rid the Islamic world of unacceptable regimes might be a long-term endeavour, but humbling the far enemy in Afghanistan would have been a tremendous aid to recruitment and the gaining of more general support.

Iraq and the War on Terror

It is useful to summarise the hopes and intentions of the two main parties to the war on terror. From an American perspective, Afghanistan and Iraq would make the transition to peaceful pro-western market economies with a long-term US military presence providing regime security if required. The al-Qaida movement would be in retreat and Iran would accept US security dominance in its immediate region and would not therefore challenge such dominance. From the perspective of al-Qaida, the United States would have experienced a dramatic attack on its own soil, with all the propaganda results that this would entail, and might well be drawn into occupying Afghanistan, with the likely development of an insurgency. From such perspectives it is appropriate to review the developments of the past five years with particular reference to the period from May 2005 to April 2006 to see how these aspirations were reflected in actual developments.

Afghanistan
Although the termination of the Taliban regime in Afghanistan was achieved with relative ease, the security support and the developmental resources needed to enable Afghanistan to undergo comprehensive post-conflict reconstruction and development have not been forthcoming. It was argued by knowledgeable UN analysts that Afghanistan required the early deployment of a stabilisation force of around 30,000 troops to be sent to the country within months of the Taliban withdrawal, but this was not done. From 2002 onwards, the United States was not committed to post-conflict peace-building in Afghanistan to any substantial degree and was rapidly becoming pre-occupied with the developing insurgency in Iraq.

Over the period 2002 to 2005, there were persistent problems of insecurity in Afghanistan, especially away from the major cities such as Kabul and in the more rural areas of south and south-east Afghanistan. A pattern of insecurity developed in which most of the anti-government and anti-western activities took place during the summer months with relative pauses in activity each winter. Taliban and other militias progressively re-grouped over this period and were aided by a marked lack of control by the Pakistani government of the border districts such as North and South Waziristan. By the early part of 2006, there was a clear resurgence in Taliban capabilities, with operations being conducted on both sides of the Afghanistan/ Pakistan border that were more intense than at any time since early 2002.

In eastern Afghanistan a force of around 20,000 US personnel has been engaged in an open counter-insurgency campaign against Taliban and other elements, even if this has attracted little attention in the western media. Elsewhere in the country NATO assumed the leadership of ISAF, and member states have been putting in place significant numbers of troops in roles that were intended initially to be in support of stabilisation. However, by the early summer of 2006, NATO/ ISAF forces such as the large British contingent in Helmand province in southern Afghanistan were increasingly engaged in direct counter-insurgency operations rather than a 'hearts and minds' policy as had originally been envisaged.

Three aspects of the Taliban revival are of particular significance. One is that they maintained a relatively high level of activity over the winter of 2005–06 – indeed this was the first winter since 2001–02 where there were substantial problems of insecurity and Taliban activity across much of the country. The second aspect is that large numbers of Taliban and other militias, sometimes allied with local warlords, have been able to take control of rural areas and act with impunity except when ISAF or US patrols are in the vicinity. Finally, there is growing evidence of the increasing opposition to western forces of Afghans, at least away from cities such as Kabul.

American and European forces are even beginning to be seen as foreign occupiers, in the same manner as the Soviet Union's forces were over 20 years earlier.

In part this has been due to the very vigorous pursuit of insurgents by US forces – their tendency to use ground- and air-based firepower frequently resulting in civilian casualties.

Iraq

As detailed in Chapter 1, in the first two years of the Iraq War, what had been expected to be rapid regime termination followed by an early and substantial withdrawal of the majority of the US forces and the transition to a pro-western government in Baghdad was transformed into an evolving insurgency that proved very costly to Iraqis and to coalition forces especially those of the United States. With the war now into its fourth year, the civilian casualties within Iraq are at least 45,000 killed and perhaps 100,000 injured, with these being base-line figures from published sources. As such they are likely to be severe underestimates of the true losses.

In June 2006 it was reported that there had been about 6,000 civilians killed in Baghdad alone in the first five months of the year, approximately double the number killed in the same period in 2005. Virtually every western journalist with long-term experience of the country has reported a marked deterioration in the levels of security. In addition to the huge numbers of deaths and injuries, the economy is in a parlous state and repeated attacks by insurgents have resulted in very low levels of oil revenues, as well as fuel shortages, huge disruption to electricity supplies and levels of unemployment typically exceeding 50 per cent. Progress in forming a permanent and stable Iraqi administration has been far slower than expected, one example in the first part of 2006 being a five-month delay in even forming a government.

During the course of the past three years there have been many occasions when particular events have been hailed as marking the end, or at least the easing, of the insurgency. These have included the deaths of Qusay and Uday Hussein in July 2003, the detention of Saddam Hussein in December 2003, the transition from the US-controlled Coalition Provisional Authority to an appointed Iraqi administration in June 2004, the assault on the supposed insurgent centre of Fallujah in November 2004, elections and the formation of a constitution in 2005 and the death of a prominent insurgent, the Jordanian Abu Musab al-Zarqawi, in June 2006.

Instead, the insurgency has continued and evolved, often with new weapons and tactics being used, such as shaped-charge explosives and infra-red detonation of improvised explosive devices. Over the period since the start of the war, the United States has lost over 2,500 of its service personnel killed and, as of mid-June 2006, over 19,000 injured, half of them sustaining serious injuries with many evacuated back to the United States for long-term treatment. In addition, at least 25,000 US troops have been evacuated from Iraq because of non-combat injuries, physical or mental ill health.

During the period under review in this annual report, May 2005 to April 2006, domestic support for the war in the United States fell substantially, partly because of the rising casualties, but incidents of prisoner abuse, especially at the Abu Ghraib prison, also had their effect. As US forces moved into the fourth year of the war, there were clear indications of an intention to stay for the long term, including major construction projects under way at four large air bases. Moreover, this period also witnessed a shift in tactics towards the greater use of air power in confronting the insurgency. During the calendar year 2005, the daily rate of air strikes against insurgents increased fivefold. Even if this resulted in a decrease in ground patrols, the effect on US casualty rates was minimal, and one inevitable effect was the increase in civilian casualties.

The US perspective

If a comparison is drawn between US expectations in early 2002 and the reality in mid-2006, then in every respect the security situation has been substantially worse than expected. Afghanistan is witnessing an upsurge in violence and a resurgence of the Taliban and allied groups, Iraq remains mired in a bitter insurgency, and the al-Qaida movement and its dispersed associates remain active, not least with attacks over the past year in Sinai, London, Bali, Aqaba, Karachi and Amman.

One major response of the Bush administration has been to emphasise the connection between the Iraq War and its wider global war on terror, citing Iraq as the current focus of that war with the advantageous result that al-Qaida is being confronted in Iraq rather than the United States. One effect of this approach is that it continues the process of linking Iraq with al-Qaida, an aspect of the Bush administration's presentation of the war that has been followed right from the start. Indeed, even before the military action against the Saddam Hussein regime started in March 2003, the administration made this connection, although there was little evidence to support it. The value of the approach lies in diverting attention from the other stated motive for regime termination, Iraq's presumed development of weapons of mass destruction.

The Al-Qaida Perspective

In one sense, the American emphasis on the Iraq/al-Qaida connection has been akin to a self-fulfilling prophecy as young jihadists have travelled to Iraq from Saudi Arabia, Yemen, Egypt, Algeria and even Afghanistan to aid the insurgency and gain direct combat experience. Although such people make up less than one-tenth of the total number of insurgents, their presence is a considerable asset for the wider al-Qaida movement. In historical perspective, Afghanistan in the 1980s became a combat training zone for jihadists as the US-supported resistance opposed the Soviet occupation in the last major confrontation of the Cold War era. In the 1990s, the Afghan civil war between the Taliban and the Northern Alliance again provided a wider jihadist focus. This was lost, at least for a few years until the Taliban resurgence in 2006, but has now been replaced by Iraq.

In other respects the al-Qaida perspective is less positive. The United States did not get immediately mired in Afghanistan following the 9/11 attacks, even if there is a marked Taliban revival now under way. The al-Qaida movement is not making much progress in changing regimes in Saudi Arabia or other Middle Eastern states, even if there is always the possibility of sudden regime change in Pakistan. While its support is probably stronger than five years ago, as part of a more general increase in anti-Americanism, al-Qaida can hardly be said to have awakened a mass movement across the Islamic world.

At the same time, it is a movement that measures its aims in decades through to a century and, in this respect, it differs markedly from political change in the United States where policy is configured primarily in terms of short-term electoral timescales, even if neo-conservatives have talked in terms of an American Century. What is relevant, however, is the transition of thinking in influential circles in the United States from a war on terror to the Long War, as discussed in Chapter 13, with this being seen as replacing the Cold War with perhaps a similar duration.

Endless War

In essence, the al-Qaida movement may not have had the successes that it would have wished but the developments in Iraq and Afghanistan during 2005–06, coupled with continued activities elsewhere, have demonstrated that the United States has faced greater reversals in its pursuit of its global war on terror or long war. In any case, the al-Qaida movement is engaged in a very long-term process with strong revolutionary elements. It will not be diverted from this process unless its very support withers away over time.

The United States may be guided by short-term political factors, but its military planners and their political masters have now embraced the idea of a long conflict, the Long War, and show no signs of re-thinking policy. This may well be dictated in part by the importance to United States administrations of the security of Israel within the Middle East.

Israel's role in the Bush administration's global war on terror came to the fore in July 2006 with the start of Israel's extensive military actions in Lebanon. Although this was essentially about seeking the curbing and disarming of the Hezbollah militias, it was seen from Washington as a core part of the much wider conflict. There remains a widespread belief within the Bush administration that Iran is the major focus of the axis of evil, and this extends to the belief that Iran is deeply implicated in security problems in Iraq and even Afghanistan. It follows, from a US perspective, that the role of Hezbollah as a surrogate for the Iranian regime has been a core problem within the phenomenon of international terrorism, making it essential to offer the fullest support possible for Israel.

Even a few weeks into the Lebanon War, however, it was apparent that the heavy civilian casualties were adding hugely to the anti-American and anti-Israeli mood across the Middle East. The al-Qaida movement sought to benefit from this, even if the connections between Hezbollah and al-Qaida have been regarded by most analysts as minimal.

Beyond this conflict, though, there still lies the enduring importance of the Persian Gulf oil resources, with both the United States and China increasingly relying on the region, which means that it would be entirely unacceptable for the

United States to consider withdrawal from Iraq, no matter how insecure the environment.

At some stage it is likely that there will be a fundamental re-assessment of the pursuit of the Long War. This will have to extend to considering alternatives to the current military posture, including the development of policies that seek to undercut support for the diverse aims of the al-Qaida movement. At the time of writing that seems unlikely. Nor does it appear probable that the 2008 Presidential election campaign will be an occasion for such a consideration. At the same time, if the predicaments facing the United States and its coalition partners in Iraq and Afghanistan both worsen, then such a re-assessment may well begin. The fourth year of the Iraq War and the sixth year of the Afghanistan War might determine that, but in the process there are likely to be many casualties and much suffering.

Sustainable Security and Global Issues

The current US security paradigm is essentially one of 'control' – a matter of responding to current and potential threats primarily by the use of military force. Five years after 9/11 this is being shown to be increasingly ineffective within the context of the responses to those attacks, but the greater criticism is that it embodies a mindset that is wholly inappropriate to responding to the major long-term causes of insecurity likely to affect the wider global community. Two issues are particularly important, both tending to interact with processes of global militarisation that assume military responses to political problems.

A core feature of the evolving global economy is the highly variable distribution of economic growth, with perhaps one fifth of the global population experiencing substantial increases in wealth but drawing rapidly away from the remaining four-fifths. While abject poverty may not be increasing, most of the world's peoples are not sharing in the effects of economic growth, yet the welcome improvements in education, literacy and communications all mean that there is a much greater knowledge of the extent of the marginalisation of most people from the minority elite communities. There are many consequences, not least in increases in criminality, especially in urban communities, but a particularly significant consequence is a tendency towards radical and sometimes violent social movements, such as the Maoist rebellion in Nepal, the rebirth of the Naxa movements in India and, to an extent, elements of radical Islamic movements.

Allied to the issue of deepening global inequalities is the developing phenomenon of environmental constraints on human activity, not least in terms of intensifying competition for diminishing resources such as fossil fuels, the Persian Gulf being a key region for actual and potential conflict. Even more serious are the expected consequences of climate change, especially as it is recognised that future changes in rainfall patterns across heavily populated tropical regions will lead to intense migratory pressures and other forms of social unrest.

These issues present the context for global security over the next 30 years and require some fundamental moves away from 'control' security towards 'sustainable' security, with far less emphasis on maintaining control through the use of force and far more emphasis on responding to the underlying problems. This will necessarily include a fundamental redirection of efforts towards sustainable and cooperative economic development, involving comprehensive trade reform and debt relief coupled with gendered support for substantial anti-poverty programmes. It will also include a far greater commitment to the use of energy conservation and the exploitation of sustainable energy resources, both to relieve pressure on oil reserves in the short term and, even more important, to avoid the evolving problems caused by climate change.[3]

Although there is a growing recognition of the core need to address this wider agenda, such a recognition is not currently apparent in most circles of political leadership, and the responses to 9/11 have actually reinforced the current control paradigm. Given, though, that these responses are now being shown to be deeply inadequate if not directly counterproductive, it is at least possible that as a serious reappraisal begins to develop, this might go well beyond the immediate War on Terror and its evolution into a Long War. In doing so it may embrace those major issues of the twenty-first century that are likely to be far more substantial than the current preoccupation with terrorism.

Notes

Introduction

1. Paul Rogers, *Iraq: Consequences of a War*, Oxford Research Group briefing paper, October 2002.

Chapter 1   The Context for a Long War

1. Charles Krauthammer, 'The Bush Doctrine, ABM, Kyoto and the New American Unilateralism', *Weekly Standard*, 4 June 2001, Washington DC.
2. For a detailed analysis of the early weeks of the war, see, Paul Rogers, *A War Too Far: Iraq, Iran and the New American Century*, Pluto Press, London, 2006.
3. <www.iraqbodycount.net/>.
4. *Strategic Survey 2004/05*, International Institute for Strategic Studies, London, 2005.
5. Interviewed on *Newsnight*, BBC Television Channel 2, 14 June 2005.

Chapter 2   US Options in Iraq – May 2005

1. Coalition casualties in Iraq are listed at *Iraq Coalition Casualties Count*,< www.icasualties.org/oif/>. Monthly figures for deaths are listed and weekly figures for injuries are divided into two lists. One is minor injuries requiring treatment but with personnel returned to duty within 72 hours and the second is those requiring longer-term treatment. Because of the use of personal body armour and the high standards of battlefield medicine, longer-term brain trauma has been described as 'the signature wound' of the Iraq War. See Gregg Zoroya, 'Key Iraq Wound: Brain Trauma', *USA Today*, 4 March 2005. In addition, a report from the Department of Veteran Affairs in the United States indicated that 'The wars in Afghanistan and Iraq will produce a new generation of veterans at risk for the

chronic health problems that result, in part, from exposure to the stress, adversity, and trauma of war-zone experiences.' Brett T. Litz, *The Unique Circumstances and Mental Health Impact of the Wars in Afghanistan and Iraq*, National Center for Post-Traumatic Stress Disorder, Department of Veteran Affairs, Washington DC, April 2005.

2. For example, at least 50 people were killed in a suicide bomb attack on a police recruitment centre in the northern city of Irbil on 4 May. The following day a series of attacks killed at least 23 people in and around Baghdad. These included two attacks on police patrols and a bomb attack at a recruitment at the Muthanna air base near the centre of Baghdad (BBC News, 5 May 2005). By early 2005, attacks on police and army recruitment centres had become a distinguishing feature in the evolution of the insurgency.

3. Further confirmation of plans for four large bases came during May 2005. According to a senior US official in Baghdad, this had been a long-term aspect of US strategy in Iraq: 'It has always been a main plank of our exit strategy to withdraw from the urban areas as and when Iraqi forces are trained up and able to take the strain.' See Michael Howard, 'US Military to Build Four Giant New Bases in Iraq', *Guardian*, London, 23 May 2005. The emphasis on Iraqi security forces relates to the trend in the insurgency towards attacks on recruits to such forces (Note 1 above).

4. As part of a wider repositioning of US forces, it is likely that there will be an increased presence of US forces in former Warsaw Pact states, especially Romania and Bulgaria. Given political development in Turkey, especially the refusal of the Turkish Parliament to allow a US Army division to enter Iraq form Turkey in 2003, there has been increased interest in these two states bordering the Black Sea. Facilities have been used for staging purposes but there are indications that this will become a more permanent arrangement, possibly with a permanent US military headquarters presided over by a two-star general. See Vince Crawley, 'U.S. Presence Blossoms in East Europe', *Defense News*, 30 May 2005.

5. Given the continuing problems of insurgent attacks on Iraqi oil facilities, a major issue would be the role of the bases in securing oil production and distribution. An indication of the problem was the persistent claims of inadequate training and equipment for the Iraqi pipeline security team for the 480-km Kirkuk–Ceyhan pipeline. This 1,500-strong team lost its commanding officer and eleven other guards in an attack in April, 2005, and further attacks in May. Prior to the start of the war, the pipeline typically carried 800,000 barrels of oil per day, but this had been reduced to 100,000 barrels per day because of sabotage. See Nawal Athneel, 'Oil Route Under

Constant Threat', *Iraq Crisis Report No 126*, Institute for War and Peace Reporting, London, 25 May 2005.

Chapter 3   Iraq, Afghanistan and US Public Opinion – June 2005

1. Unusually, the Iraqi Interior Ministry released figures for Iraqi civilians killed in the past 18 months of the insurgency at 12,000. See Ellen Knickmeyer, 'Iraq Puts Civilian Toll at 12,000', *Washington Post*, 3 June 2005. The statement suggested that these casualties had resulted from attacks by insurgents, whereas other detailed compilations from external agencies indicated a large proportion of the casualties were due to action by coalition forces, especially US soldiers. See for example, the Iraq Body Count group that has compiled data from multiple cross-checked media sources. <www.iraqbodycount.net/>.

2. 'Rumsfeld: Iraq Insurgency Could Last Years', Associated Press, 27 June 2005.

3. Rumsfeld's views were endorsed by US military commanders in Iraq. According to Brigadier General Donald Alston, chief military spokesperson in Iraq, 'I think the more accurate way to approach this right now is to concede that ... this insurgency is not going to be settled, the terrorists and the terrorism are not going to be settled, through military options or military operations. It's going to be settled in the political process.' See Tom Lasseter, 'Officers Say Arms Can't End Iraq War', Knight Ridder Newspapers, 13 June 2005.

4. As the insurgency evolved, the tensions within Iraq increased as sectarian issues caused further delays in developing the committee to write the permanent constitution. See Jonathan Finer and Naseer Nouri, 'Sectarian Divide Widens on Iraq's Constitutional Panel', *Washington Post*, 9 June 2005.

5. Carlotta Gall, 'Despite Years of U.S. Pressure, Taliban Fight on in Jagged Hills', *New York Times*, 4 June 2005.

6. There were occasional media reports of an Afghanistan/Iraq connection prior to June 2005, but a more detailed assessment of the long-term implications of this trend was made by the Central Intelligence Agency and distributed internally in May 2005. According to one report, this said 'Iraq may prove to be an even more effective training ground for Islamic extremists than Afghanistan was in Al Qaeda's early days, because it is serving as a real-world laboratory for urban combat.' See Douglas Jehl, 'Iraq May Be Prime Place for Training of Militants, CIA Report Concludes', *New York Times*, 22 June 2005.

7. 'Taleban Capture Afghan District', Aljazeera.net, 18 June 2005.

8. In spite of the use of helicopter gun-ships and fixed-wing strike aircraft by US forces, there were warnings of further instability, including a statement to the UN Security Council from the UN's most senior diplomat in Afghanistan, Jena Arnault, which said that 'The country is confronted with an escalation of both the number and gravity of incidents that affect several provinces.' <www.newsvote.bbc.co.uk/>.
9. Ann Scott Tyson, 'Army Aims to Catch up on Recruits in Summer', *Washington Post*, 11 June 2005.
10. The Army failed to meet its recruitment targets in May for the fourth month in a row and was faced with signing up almost half of its annual recruitment total in the remaining four months of Fiscal Year 2005. This was in spite of taking on a thousand more recruiting staff, increasing enlistment cash bonuses to $20,000, spending $200 million on recruitment advertisements and lowering entry standards. See Joseph L. Galloway, 'Army Lowers Standards, Raises Perks', Knight Ridder Newspapers, 14 June 2005.

Chapter 4   London, Sharm al-Sheikh and the al-Qaida movement – July 2005

1. This stance was rather undermined by an analysis stemming from research conducted as part of the New Security Challenges Programme (SCP) of the UK Economic and Social Research Council (ESRC). Contrary to the UK government's view, one conclusion of the study was that 'The UK is at particular risk because it is the closest ally of the United States, has deployed armed forces in the military campaigns to topple the Taleban regime in Afghanistan and in Iraq, and has taken a leading role in international intelligence, police and judicial cooperation against Al-Qaeda and in efforts to suppress its finances. Al-Qaeda's taped propaganda messages have repeatedly threatened attacks on the UK.' Furthermore: 'There is no doubt that the situation over Iraq has imposed particular difficulties for the UK, and for the wider coalition against terrorism. It gave a boost to the Al-Qaeda network's propaganda, recruitment and fundraising, caused a major split in the coalition, provided an ideal targeting and training area for Al-Qaeda-linked terrorists, and deflected resources and assistance that could have been deployed to assist the Karzai government and to bring bin Laden to justice.' See Frank Gregory and Paul Wilkinson, 'Riding Pillion for Tackling Terrorism is a High-risk Policy', *Security, Terrorism and the UK*, ISP/NSC Briefing Paper 05/01, Chatham House and Economic and Social Research Council, July 2005.

2. *A Dossier of Civilian Casualties in Iraq, 2003–2005*. Oxford Research Group and Iraq Body Count. Available at <www.oxfordresearchgroup.org.uk/>.

3. On occasions, US British counter-terrorism specialists advocate recognising the nature of the multiple aims of the al-Qaida movement and responding by undercutting the circumstances that aid those aims. An example is a former CIA analyst, Michael Scheuer, who headed the Agency's Bin Laden unit for nine years until he resigned in November 2004. In his view, the occupation of Iraq was a major step backwards in confronting the al-Qaida movement, and he recommended US military withdrawal from the Middle East, an end to unqualified support for Israel and the severing of close links with elite leaderships of oil-rich Arab states. See 'Experts Fear "Endless" Terror War', Associated Press, 9 July 2005.

4. In recognition of the risk of al-Qaida recruiting from a wider region beyond the Middle East, the US Department of Defense is planning a seven-year $500 million initiative to train troops in a number of African countries in counter-guerrilla operations, including improved links between countries. The countries involved are Algeria, Chad, Mali, Mauritania, Niger, Senegal, Nigeria, Morocco and Tunisia. In addition to training programmes and provision of equipment, more military officers will be assigned to embassies in the countries concerned, with agreements sought to provide legal protection for such personnel. See Ann Scott Tyson, 'U.S. Pushes Anti-Terrorism in Africa', *Washington Post*, 26 July 2005.

Chapter 5   Gaza in Context – August 2005

1. According to a senior Israel Defence Force source, 'This will become Israel's most advanced and protected border.' See Alon Ben-David, 'Israel Bolsters Border with Gaza', *Jane's Defence Weekly*, 21 September 2005.

2. In one of the most costly incidents in the war, 14 Marines and an interpreter were killed when their assault vehicle was destroyed by a large bomb near Haditha, following the deaths of six other Marines in the same area two days earlier. CNN, 'Fourteen Marines Killed in Bombing', 3 August 2005. According to US military sources, the Iraqi insurgency does not follow the typical pattern of a centralised, hierarchically organised system. Instead, 'Vast numbers of small, adaptive insurgent cells operate independently without central guidance. There may be some loose coordination of attacks, but then the cells go their separate ways. This highly decentralized characteristic of the IED cells makes them nearly impossible to penetrate.' See Greg Grant, 'Inside Iraqi Insurgent Cells', *Defense News*, 1 August 2005.

3. During the course of August, US domestic opposition to the war in Iraq grew substantially, much of it focused on the presence of Cindy Sheehan, the mother of a soldier killed in Iraq, in a peace camp close to President Bush's ranch in Crawford, Texas. At the end of the month Bush sought to counter this mood, making a speech at a Naval Air Station to commemorate the 1945 victory over Japan. On this occasion he put forward a new reason for maintaining a vigorous US presence in Iraq – the need to prevent an oil-rich failing state falling into the hands of Islamist terrorists. This followed a marked tendency by US sources in Iraq to centre much of the insurgency on the Jordanian, Abu Musab al-Zarqawi, and his presumed links with the al-Qaida movement. According to Bush: 'If Zarqawi and bin Laden gain control of Iraq, they would create a new training ground for future terrorist attacks. They'd seize oil fields to fund their ambitions. They could recruit more terrorists by claiming a historic victory over the United States and our coalition.' See Jennifer Loven, 'Bush Gives New Reason for Iraq War', Associated Press, 31 August 2005.

4. One of many examples was the killing of 25 Iraqi Army recruits and the wounding of 35 others by a suicide bomber who managed to get into a high security area being used as a recruitment depot in the town of Rabia, north-west of Mosul. 'Bomb Kills 25 Army Recruits', BBC News, 1 August 2005.

5. The increased use of air power against the insurgents was a developing feature of US tactics in the early months of 2005, with coalition combat aircraft flying about 50 close-air support and armed reconnaissance missions every day. Furthermore, there was a strong view within the US Air Force that air support for Iraqi security forces would involve a long-term USAF presence and involvement in the country. According to General John P. Jumper, the retiring Air Force Chief of Staff: 'We will continue with a rotational presence of some type in that area more or less indefinitely. We have interests in that part of the world and an interest in staying in touch with the militaries over there.' See Eric Schmitt, 'U.S. General Says Iraqis Will Need Longtime Support From Air Force', *New York Times*, 30 August 2005.

6. The use of the Web by the al-Qaida movement has expanded rapidly, with a wide range of web pages available, designed for distribution in numerous versions ranging from high capacity, high speed communication down to basic versions that can be downloaded to mobile phones. See Susan B. Glasser and Steve Coll, 'The Web as Weapon', *Washington Post*, 9 August 2005.

Chapter 6   The US Military and the 'War on Terror' –
            September 2005

1. David Brunnstrom, 'US Troop Deaths Take Afghan Toll This Year
   above 50', Reuters, 27 September 2005.
2. Tensions were reported with the Afghan President, Hamid Karzai,
   over US military tactics in the Afghan counter-insurgency. Mr Karzai
   expressed concern at the repeated house to house searches by US
   soldiers and the frequent use of air power, and sought a change
   in military operations towards a more cautious approach. 'Karzai
   renews terror rethink plea', BBC News, 23 September 2005.
3. An indication of insurgent capabilities was a daylight raid on
   the heavily protected Interior Ministry in central Baghdad on 5
   September. Four carloads of insurgents attacked the ministry building
   using rocket propelled grenades and automatic weapons. In the 15-
   minute attack, two police were killed and five wounded before the
   insurgents escaped, with no casualties reported. See Slobodan Lekic,
   'Iraqi Rebels Launch Daring Daylight Assault', *Associated Press*, 5
   September 2005. 'Iraqi fighters launch deadly attacks', Aljazeera.
   net, 5 September 2005.
4. In September 2004, a large force of US and Iraqi troops took control
   of the city of Tal Afar, later withdrawing to leave behind a force of
   500 troops to patrol the city and a large surrounding area. Insurgents
   returned in the following months and took control, and the new
   operation, a year later, involved 5,000 US and Iraqi troops, the
   largest operation since the Fallujah assault in November 2004. See
   Jonathan Finer, '5,000 U.S. and Iraqi Troops Sweep Into City of Tal
   Afar', *Washington Post*, 3 September 2005. However, within six
   days of the start of the operation, it was reported that: 'Insurgents
   staged a classic guerrilla retreat from Tal Afar on Sunday, melting
   into the countryside through a network of tunnels to escape an
   Iraqi–U.S. force that reported killing about 150 rebels while storming
   the militant bastion.' See 'Death Toll Mounts in Tal Afar', Associated
   Press, 11 September 2005. Moreover, almost simultaneous with this
   operation, insurgents took control of the town of Qaim close to the
   Syrian border. See Ellen K. Nickmeyer and Jonathan Finer, 'Insurgents
   Assert Control over Town Near Syrian Border', *Washington Post*, 6
   September 2005.
5. A measure of the problems in Iraq was an assessment published
   in Washington quoting a range of Iraqi and Qatar-based analysts,
   reporting a steady escalation in the violence in Iraq towards a civil
   war. See Riad Kahwaji, 'Things Are Getting Worse By the Day',
   Defense News, 5 September 2005.

Chapter 7   Iraq in a Wider Perspective – October 2005

1. 'Deadly Blasts Rock Baghdad Hotels', BBC News, 25 October 2005.
2. The form of shaped charge explosive in use in Iraq utilises a small concave-shaped copper piece which, with its low melting point, is fashioned by an explosive charge into a high velocity molten slug that penetrates armour. See Greg Grant, 'Inside Iraqi Insurgent Cells', *Defense News*, 1 August 2005. There are suggestions that such technology has come into the hands of insurgents from Syrian or Iranian sources, but the Saddam Hussein regime had its own expertise and the technology may also be indigenous.
3. In one action near Ramadi, 70 people were reported killed by air attacks by US strike aircraft and helicopter gun-ships. US sources reported that all those killed were insurgents, including a group said to be emplacing a roadside bomb close to where five US soldiers had died earlier. Local Iraqi sources disputed this, saying that 25 of those killed were civilians who were standing round the wreckage from the earlier attack, some of them scavenging equipment. 'US Strikes Kill "70 Iraq rebels"', BBC News, 17 October 2005.
4. Peter Baker and Susan B. Glasser, 'Bush Says 10 Plots by Al Qaeda Were Foiled', *Washington Post*, 7 October 2005.
5. Furthermore, there are indications that an al-Qaida/Taliban nexus has been re-established in Afghanistan, with support in parts of Pakistan, as a result of which, US and Pakistani officials are seeking to work out a new consensus strategy. See Syed Saleem Shahzad, 'US Back to the Drawing Board in Afghanistan', *Asia Times*, 6 October 2005. One of the problems is the delicate political position of the Pakistani leader, General Musharraf – quite widespread domestic opposition to the United States and support for radical Islamists means that cooperation between Pakistan and the United States tends to increase political tensions within Pakistan.
6. Whatever the eventual configuration of US forces in Iraq, there has been a notable change in administration rhetoric, from an earlier position that al-Qaida and similar paramilitary groups would lose influence in the region as democracy took hold. Instead, Mr Bush 'has begun warning that the insurgency is already metastasising into a far broader struggle to "establish a radical Islamic empire that spans from Spain to Indonesia"'. See David E. Sanger, 'Administration's Tone Signals a Longer, Broader Conflict', *New York Times*, 17 October 2005.
7. The head of the Canadian Security Intelligence Service was one of a number of established security professionals to take the view that the US-led war in Iraq is having a negative impact on international security, describing Iraq as a 'kind of test bed for new techniques'.

See Jim Bronskill, 'War in Iraq May Be Fuelling Global Insecurity, Canadian Spy Chief Warns', The Canadian Press, 20 October 2005.

Chapter 8   The Politics of War – November 2005

1. Sara Daniel and Sami Yousafzay, 'Terrorism: The Return of the Taliban', Le Nouvel Observateur, 3 November 2005.
2. Following the multiple bomb attacks in Amman, there were indications that the Jordanian guerrilla leader, Abu Musab al-Zarqawi, was involved, although there have also been concerns that the US authorities tend to focus on individuals such as Zarqawi, elevating them to an importance they do not warrant. See Craig Whitlock, 'Amman Bombings Reflect Zarqawi's Growing Reach', Washington Post, 13 November 2005.
3. The KFC attack coincided with the hearing of an appeal against the death sentence on Ahgmed Omar Saeed Sheikh, convicted earlier of the kidnap and murder of Daniel Pearl, an American journalist. See 'Car Bomb Hits Karachi restaurant', BBC News, 15 November 2005. The KFC outlet was in a supposedly secure business district of Karachi, close to two international hotels. In addition to other smaller attacks on western-linked businesses, Karachi has previously been the scene of attacks on the US consulate and a group of French naval technicians.
4. 'Influential Democratic Hawk Calls for Immediate Iraq Exit', Associated Press, 17 November 2005. Concern over the deteriorating situation in Iraq also led Congressional Republicans to call on the Bush administration to set out a strategy for ending the war. See Carl Hulse, 'Senate Republicans Pushing for a Plan on Ending War in Iraq', New York Times, 15 November 2005.
5. 'Bush Outlines Iraq "Victory Plan"', BBC News, 30 November 2005. The plan comprised a 'Victory in Iraq' document released alongside a speech by President Bush at the US Naval Academy at Annapolis, Maryland. See National Strategy for Victory in Iraq, National Security Council, Washington DC, November 2005.
6. While recognising the status of Jack Murtha as a Vietnam veteran, neo-conservative commentators sought to point out the consequences of a withdrawal from Iraq. For example: Robert Kagan and William Kristol, 'Abandoning Iraq: does Rep. Murtha understand the consequences of immediate withdrawal from Iraq?' The Weekly Standard, 28 November 2005. Comments on criticisms of the conduct of the war by Republican members of Congress were far more antagonistic: William Kristol, 'Pathetic, the me-too Republicans wimp out on Iraq', The Weekly Standard, 15 November 2005.

7. With the mid-sessional elections to Congress barely a year away, the administration sought once again to link the war in Iraq with the wider war on terror and therefore with the 9/11 attacks. Vice-President Dick Cheney was particularly strong in promoting this view in response to pressure to pull out US troops from Iraq, stating that 'It is a dangerous illusion to suppose that another retreat by the civilized world would satisfy the appetite of the terrorists and get them to leave us alone.' He further asserted: 'Now they're making a stand in Iraq, testing our resolve, trying to intimidate the United States into abandoning our friends and permitting the overthrow of this new Middle East democracy.' See Douglass K. Daniel, 'Cheney Attempts to Tie Iraq to 9–11 Again', Associated Press, 21 November 2005.

Chapter 9   Control without the Consequences – December 2005

1. There was an assumption that troop reductions might therefore be possible but not all US military sources agreed on the feasibility of this. One significant note of caution was an interview given by Marines General Peter Pace, Chair of the Joint Chiefs of Staff, to Fox TV News on Christmas Day, when he agreed that there could even be troop increases dependent on the changing nature of the insurgency: 'So if things go the way we expect them to, as more Iraqi units stand up, we'll be able to bring our troops down and turn over that territory to the Iraqis. But on the other hand, the enemy has a vote in this, and if they were to cause some kind of problems that required more troops, then we would do exactly what we've done in the past, which is give the commanders on the ground what they need. And in that case you could see troop level go up a little bit to handle that problem.' See Josh Meyer, 'Military Leader Says Troop Level Could Rise', Los Angeles Times, 26 December 2005.

2. Neo-conservative analysts, in particular, remained adamant that all necessary resources had to be put into the conflict to ensure victory. See, for example, Tom Donnelly, 'The Goal is Victory', The Weekly Standard, 1 December 2005, and: Frederick W. Kagan, 'Fighting to Win', The Weekly Standard, 19 December 2005.

3. In one of the worst incidents, earlier in December, a roadside bomb made from several artillery shells killed 10 Marines on a foot patrol and injured eleven others. The attack happened on the outskirts of Fallujah, demonstrating once again that the assault on the city and the subsequent subjugation of the insurgency there had been short-lived. See Jonathan Finer, '10 Marines Killed in Fallujah

Blast, Incidents Temper View of City's Progress', *Washington Post*, 3 December 2005.

4. Even so, there remained substantial concerns about developments in Afghanistan. Taliban paramilitaries are reported to have gained access to new supplies of weapons including modern automatic weapons and ground-to-air missiles. This has involved improved links with groups in Iraq as well as linkages with the LTTE (Tamil Tigers) in Sri Lanka. See Syed Saleem Shahzad, 'Armed and Dangerous: Taliban Gear Up', *Asia News*, 21 December 2005. There have also been concerns about the drug economy. Although there was a slight decline in poppy cultivation in 2004–05 compared with 2003–04, there were indications that productivity was increased so that net production of opium was scarcely below the previous year's figures, with early indications of increased plantings likely, not least because the hundreds of millions of dollars put into anti-drug programmes has had little effect. See Andrew North, 'Losing the War on Afghan Drugs', BBC News, 22 December 2005. Furthermore, there were more general concerns over US tactics in Afghanistan, coupled with doubts over the capacity of the new Afghan National Army to take over security duties and concerning the ability of the Pakistani armed forces to control the border regions. See Andrew North, 'Doubts Grow Over US Afghan Strategy', BBC News, 22 December 2005.

5. In these circumstances, concern over the effectiveness of US information efforts has led to a $300 million psychological warfare operation that 'includes plans for placing pro-American messages in foreign media outlets without disclosing the US government as the source, one of the military officials in charge of the program says'. The programme will be run throughout the world by the Joint Psychological Operations Support Element of US Special Operations Command. See Matt Kelley, 'Pentagon Rolls Out Stealth PR', *USA Today*, 14 December 2005.

Chapter 10   *Iraq, Afghanistan and now Iran Once Again – January 2006*

1. A major problem with handing over to Iraqi troops was the issue of reliability. In one instance, US troops handed over Saddam Hussein's most lavish complex of palaces, in Tikrit, to local security forces in a ceremony in which the US commander, Colonel Mark McKnight, said 'The passing of this facility is a simple ceremony that vividly demonstrates the continuing progress being made by the Iraqi government and their people.' Within days of the handover, the complex had been comprehensively looted, even down to doors and light fittings, leaving the 136 buildings little more than shells.

Moreover, those responsible were primarily the very security forces that had taken over from the US military. See Ellen Knickmeyer, 'After Handover, Hussein Palaces Looted', *Washington Post*, 13 January 2006.

2. The increased use of air power in counter-insurgency operations was particularly apparent in the latter part of 2005. Until August, the number averaged 25 but increased to 120 in November and was expected to rise to 150 during December. See Sarah Baxter, Ali Rifat and Peter Almond, 'US Forces Step Up Iraq Airstrikes', *Sunday Times*, London, 1 January 2006. As US troops operate increasingly from a smaller number of larger bases, the use of air power is expected to increase further. See Drew Brown, 'US Airstrikes in Iraq Could Intensify', Knight Ridder Newspapers, 11 January 2006.

3. Carlotta Gall and Mohammad Kahn, 'Pakistan's Push on Border Areas is Said to Falter', *New York Times*, 22 January 2006.

4. Griff Witte and Kamran Khan, 'U.S. Strike On Al Qaeda Top Deputy Said to Fail', *Washington Post*, 15 January 2006.

5. Griff Witte and Kamran Khan, 'Attacks Strain Efforts on Terror', *Washington Post*, 23 January 2006.

6. The use of armed drones became a feature of the war on terror, with them used on at least 19 occasions in foreign countries since the 9/11 attacks. The Central Intelligence Agency was reported to be expanding the programme to a global reach, and not necessarily requiring the agreement of the heads of state of countries where they might be used. One former counter-terrorism official was quoted: 'In most cases, we need the approval of the host country to do them. However, there are a few countries where the president has decided that we can whack someone without the approval or knowledge of the host government.' See Josh Meyer, 'CIA Expands Use of Drones in Terror War', *Los Angeles Times*, 29 January 2006.

7. There was little sign of any decrease in antagonism towards the United States from Taliban groups. The Taliban leader, Mullah Mohammad Omar, was reported to have responded to a call for dialogue from Afghan President Hamid Karzai by threatening more attacks on US forces in the country. See 'Taliban Leader Vows More Attacks in Afghanistan', Reuters, 9 January 2006.

8. Reports in the German press quoting un-named intelligence sources claimed that some NATO states and governments of Saudi Arabia, Jordan, Oman and Pakistan had been informed of US military plans for operations against Iran. See 'US and Iran: Is Washington Planning a Military Strike?' *Spiegel*, 31 December 2005. President Bush's State of the Union address a month later described Iran as 'a nation now held hostage by a small clerical elite that is isolating and repressing its people. The regime in that country sponsors terrorists in the

Palestinian territories and in Lebanon, and that must come to an end. The Iranian government is defying the world with its nuclear ambitions, and the nations of the world must not permit the Iranian regime to gain nuclear weapons.' CQ Transcripts Wire, Washington DC, 31 January 2006.

9. Paul Rogers, *Iran: Consequences of a War*, Oxford Research Group Briefing Paper, Oxford, February 2006.

10. To compound the problems in Iraq, the coalition itself was dwindling in size and the Iraqi economy was experiencing further problems relating to oil production. In relation to the coalition, at its peak in 2003, 38 states contributed 50,000 troops, but by early 2006 this had decreased to 28 nations with around 20,000 troops. Ukraine and Bulgaria completed their withdrawals in December 2005, Poland was due to withdraw 600 of its 1,500 troops in March and the South Korean parliament voted to cut its deployment in Iraq from 3,200 by 1,000, with the remainder leaving in 2007. See Mark Sappenfield, 'US Allies in Iraq: Valuable but Dwindling', *Christian Science Monitor*, 4 January 2006. Concerning oil production and exports, Iraq exported 1.1 million barrels per day (bpd) in December 2005, compared with a post-regime maximum of 1.8 million bpd earlier in the year and well below the 1.8–2.5 million bpd exported by the Saddam Hussein regime under sanctions. See 'Iraq's Oil Exports Hit Lowest Level since War', Reuters, 2 January 2006.

Chapter 11   Iraq, Three Years On – February 2006

1. Although the insurgents were at different times labelled 'remnants' of the old regime, the recognition had developed that they were diverse and made up of a range of components that were variable in size and did not have a single unified organisation. 'Iraqi and American officials in Iraq say the single most important fact about the insurgency is that it consists not of a few groups but of dozens, possibly as many as 100. And it is not, as often depicted, a coherent organization whose members dutifully carry out orders from above but a far-flung collection of smaller groups that often act on their own or come together for a single attack. Each is believed to have its own leader and is free to act on its own.' See Dexter Filkin, 'Profusion of Rebel Groups Helps Them Survive in Iraq', *New York Times*, 2 December 2005. The insurgents were reported as having a particular ability to replace group leaders who might get killed, and also being able to replace insurgents who were killed with others drawn from a substantial pool of new recruits. See Greg Grant, 'Iraqi Insurgents Find Ways to Bounce Back', *Defense News*, 20 February 2006.

2. In the six days after the bombing of the Shi'a shrine in Samarra, 1,300 people were reported killed, based on statistics from morgues, with police sources estimated deaths at 1,020. Whatever the actual figures they represented one of the worst periods of violence since the first three weeks of the war in March/April 2003. See Ellen Knickmeyer and Bassam Sebti, 'Toll in Iraq's Deadly Surge: 1,300', *Washington Post*, 28 February 2006.

3. The policy of embedding journalists with military units in Iraq has continued since the start of the war. This may give journalists a very realistic indication of the problems young American soldiers are facing in dealing with a complex and largely urban insurgency, and also gives an indication of how they react under considerable pressure. See Tom Lasseter, 'Order, Peace Elusive in Iraqi City of Samarra', Knight Ridder Newspapers, 15 February 2006.

4. Substantial questions remained over the reliability of the Iraqi security forces, including the question of detention centres run by elements within the Interior Ministry loyal to the Supreme Council of the Islamic Revolution in Iraq (SCIRI). One such centre was reported as being run by the militia wing of SCIRI, the Badr organisation, and held about 170 prisoners. See Mahan Abedin, 'Badr's Spreading Web', *Asia Times*, 11 December 2005. It was also reported that Kurdish political leaders had ensured that some 10,000 members of Kurdish militias had joined Iraqi Army divisions in the north of the country: 'The soldiers said that while they wore Iraqi army uniforms they still considered themselves members of the Pershmerga – the Kurdish militia – and were awaiting orders from Kurdish leaders to break ranks. Many said they wouldn't hesitate to kill their Iraqi army comrades, especially Arabs, if a fight for an independent Kurdistan erupted.' Tom Lasseter, 'Kurds in Iraqi Army Proclaim Loyalty to Militia', Knight Ridder Newspapers, 27 December 2005.

5. Joe Galloway, 'Military Vehicles, and Lives, Take a Beating in Iraq', *Salt Lake Tribune*, 15 February 2006.

6. At the time of the publication of the Fiscal Year 2007 defence budget and the Quadrennial Defence Review, there was a sustained effort to use the term 'Long War', not least in a Pentagon document *Fighting the Long War – Military Strategy for the War on Terror.* See, for example, Rowan Scarborough, 'Military Plots a "Long War" on Terror', *Washington Times*, 20 February 2006. The Defense Secretary, Donald Rumsfeld, saw this as a potentially generational conflict similar to the Cold War. See Josh White and Ann Scott Tyson, 'Rumsfeld Offers Strategies for Current War', *Washington Post*, 3 February 2006.

Chapter 12 Iran, Sliding to War? March 2006

1. Two days before the assassination of Qari Baba, a statement was issued attributed to the Taliban leader, Mullah Omar, warning of further attacks during the spring and summer. See Amir Shah, '5 Ambushed, Killed in Eastern Afghanistan', Associated Press, 18 March 2006.

2. Analysts with a track record of accuracy considered it likely that 2006 would prove to be a period of Taliban resurgence, aided by knowledge and tactics acquired by paramilitaries who had travelled to Iraq and had engaged in training and combat. See Syed Saleem Shahzad, 'Taliban's Iraq-style Spring is Sprung', *Asia Times*, 14 March 2006.

3. A valuable source of information on a wide range of political, social, developmental and security trends is provided by the regular analysis from the British Agencies Afghanistan Group (BAAG). The March issue of the review pointed, in particular, to the difficult relationship between the Afghanistan government and the Musharraf regime in Pakistan. See *Monthly Review*, BAAG, London, March 2006. There were particularly violent incidents involving the Pakistani Army and militias in North Waziristan in the first week of March. See Aamer Ahmed Khan, 'Pakistan Fights its own "Taleban"', BBC News, 6 March 2006.

4. Following a claim by the former Iraqi Prime Minister Ayad Allawi that Iraq was already in a state of civil war, President Bush denied this strongly, holding a press conference to argue that Iraq was actually heading for a viable democracy. At the same time, he made it clear that US troops would be engaged in Iraq after the end of his Presidency at the end of 2008. See Jim VandeHei, 'Bush Says U.S. Troops Will Stay in Iraq Past '08', *Washington Post*, 22 March 2006.

5. Figures from the Department of Defense showed 616 injuries for the period 11 February to 21 March. Overall figures for the entire period from the start of military hostilities on 19 March 2003 to 21 March 2006 were 17,269 troops injured, with 7,981 listed as 'WIA Not RTD', or wounded in action, not returned to duty. The very high proportion of injuries relative to deaths is largely explained by a combination of personal protection and high standards of medical care immediately available. See Martin Sieff, 'Benchmarks: US Iraq Casualties Stay High', United Press International, 22 March 2006.

6. The first substantive reports of plans for permanent bases circulated within weeks of the termination of the Saddam Hussein regime in April 2003. See Thom Shanker and Eric Schmitt, 'Pentagon Expects Long-Term Access to Four Key Bases in Iraq', *New York Times*, 19 April 2003. In March 2006, construction at four bases continued with the Pentagon requesting some hundreds of millions of dollars

154   INTO THE LONG WAR

for emergency funding of base construction programmes, including
$110.3 million for Tallil air base, one of those cited in the *New York
Times* report. See Becky Branford, 'Iraq Bases Spur Questions Over
US Plans', BBC News, 30 March 2006.

7. While seeking the evolution of a client government backed by US
   troops in a smaller number of large bases, the Bush administration
   also announced that it would scale down the funding of Iraqi reconstruction programmes, having spent about $21 billion. The funding
   sources in future might have an international element but would
   need to come largely from Iraqi sources, especially oil revenues.
   This would prove extremely difficult given that 2003 World Bank
   estimates of $60 billion in reconstruction costs were probably now
   of the order of $70–100 billion. See William Fisher, 'Iraq Left to
   Rebuild Itself', *Asia Times*/Inter Press Service, 29 March 2006.

8. An experienced Washington analyst, Joseph Cirincione, had been
   doubtful about a US attack on Iraq early in 2003, but now recognised
   a similar build-up towards confrontation in the case of Iran. See
   Joseph Cirincione, 'Fool Me Twice', *Foreign Policy*, April 2006.

9. There was particular concern that Iranian military and intelligence
   services were already engaged in supporting some Iraqi Shi'a militia
   groups, a view expressed forcefully by the US Ambassador to Iraq,
   Zalmay Khalilzad. See Jonathan Finer and Ellen Knickmeyer,
   'Envoy Accuses Iran of Duplicity on Iraq', *Washington Post*, 24
   March 2006.

10. A further complication is that attempts to finance and otherwise
    support opposition groups within Iran might be opposed by some
    of the groups because of a reluctance to be seen as supported by
    the United States. See Karl Vick and David Finkel, 'U.S. Push for
    Democracy Could Backfire Inside Iraq', *Washington Post*, 14 March
    2006.

Chapter 13   From Cold War to Long War – April 2006

1. Daniel Williams, 'Blasts at Sinai Resort Kill at Least 23', *Washington
   Post*, 25 April 2006.

2. While much of the press coverage of the insurgency has understand-
   ably been on the deaths of civilians, the issue of kidnapping has
   attracted less attention unless the victims are foreign. A report by a
   group of Iraqi non-governmental organisations published in April
   gave a figure of over 19,500 kidnappings since the start of the year,
   with 2,350 of them children. Most of the kidnappings were because
   of political rivalries or common criminality for ransoms. The latter,
   in particular, illustrated the low level of security offered by police

forces. See '20,000 Kidnapped in Iraq Since January: Report', Agence France-Presse, 20 April 2006.

3. A major difficulty for the US military authorities has been the rise to prominence of Shi'a militias. Following the bombing of the Shi'a shrine in Samarra in February, there was a substantial increase in killings by Shi'a gangs targeting Sunni Arabs, especially in Baghdad. According to one report, 'Assassinations, many carried out by Shiite gunmen against Sunni Arabs in Baghdad and elsewhere, accounted for four times as many deaths in March as bombings and other mass-casualty attacks, according to military data. And most officials agree that only a small percentage of shooting deaths are ever reported.' Jonathan Finer, 'Threat of Shiite Militias Now Seen As Iraq's Most Critical Challenge', *Washington Post*, 8 April 2006. The US Ambassador to Iraq, Zalmay Khalilzad, focused on the Mahdi Army, under its leader Moqtada al-Sadr, with its links to Iran, for particular attention. See Gareth Porter, 'US Anti-Militia Strategy Another Wrong Iraq Move', *Asia Times*/Inter Press Service, 4 April 2006. In one US military response, a mosque and surrounding buildings in a Shi'a district of Baghdad was targeted in March for an attack, US sources describing it as a militia centre. While there has undoubtedly been a substantial increase in Shi'a militia activity, and some may well have links with Iran, a forceful US response to these militias risks increasing the antipathy of the majority Shi'a population to the occupation.

4. One illuminating example of the problems of reconstruction was a report that a contract for the reconstruction of 142 primary health centres across Iraq let to a US construction company for $200 million had run out of money with only 20 clinics completed. An earlier report from the US Auditor for Reconstruction indicated that only 300 of 425 electricity projects and 49 out of 136 water and sanitation projects would be completed. Throughout the process security has been a major and costly issue, doing much to explain excessive costs and failures to complete. See Ellen Knickmeyer, 'U.S. Plan to Build Iraq Clinics Falters', *Washington Post*, 3 April 2006.

5. In spite of the shift to the use of air power, a major limitation has been the vulnerability of helicopters to small-arms fire. This has included the US Army's main attack helicopter, the AH-64 Apache, and, as a result, such helicopters are less likely to be used in the deep attack role, with more use being made of high-flying fixed-wing strike aircraft and long-range artillery, even though this can entail an increase in collateral damage and civilian casualties. See Greg Grant, 'U.S. Cuts Role of Apache for Deep Attack', *Defense News*, 3 April 2006.

6. One of the features of the developing conflict in Afghanistan is the increased use of roadside bombs and suicide bombs, with coordinated attacks also becoming more common. An example of the latter was an attack in the city of Kandahar on 9 April that injured 14 people. A first roadside bomb targeted an Afghan army vehicle and a second device exploded shortly afterwards as soldiers and civilians gathered at the site of the first attack. See 'Afghanistan Hit by Triple Bombing', BBC News, 9 April 2006. Three days earlier one person was killed and three injured in an explosion near the large US base at Bagram north of Kabul, and the day after that an Italian base was attacked near Heart, killing a guard and two civilians. US reaction to the increased tempo of attacks was robust, but also involved an increase in civilian casualties. In the three days to 18 April, for example, more than 20 Afghan civilians were reported killed or injured by US and Afghan security forces. See Carlotta Gall, 'Afghan Battles See Higher Toll for Civilians', *New York Times*, 19 April 2006.

7. The Pentagon's perception of a Long War was reported to be shared by the al-Qaida movement. Osama bin Laden spoke to his followers of the need to wage a 'long war' the day before the Dahab attack, warning of a western plan to occupy the Darfur region of western Sudan. The day after the Dahab attack, Abu Musab al-Zarqawi in Iraq issued a message along similar lines. See Ehsan Ahrari, 'Loud and Clear: No Respite in the "Long War"', *Asia Times*, 26 April 2006. In one sense, the wider al-Qaida aim of seeking to re-establish an Islamic Caliphate has long been seen in terms of struggle developing over decades rather than years.

Chapter 14   Endless War

1. See Chapter 1.
2. The campaign for regime change in Iraq prior to 2000, is analysed by Nick Ritchie in: Nick Ritchie and Paul Rogers, *The Political Road to War*, Routledge, Abingdon, 2006.
3. A preliminary discussion of global trends and the requirement for sustainable security is in: Chris Abbott, Paul Rogers and John Sloboda, *Global Responses to Global Threats: Sustainable Security for the 21ˢᵗ Century*, Oxford Research Group Briefing Paper, June 2006, Oxford.

Index